HOW **NOT** TO MAKE A SHORT FILM

HOW NOT TO MAKE A SHORT FILM

SECRETS FROM A SUNDANCE PROGRAMMER

Roberta Marie Munroe

HYPERION

NEW YORK

Hyperion
Hachette Book Group
237 Park Avenue
New York, NY 10017

Library of Congress Cataloging-in-Publication is available upon request.

ISBN: 978-1-4013-0954-1

Design by Pauline Neuwirth, Neuwirth & Associates, Inc.

FIRST EDITION

10   9   8   7   6   5   4

QUAD-M

For all the filmmakers of the world—
here's to building our empires.
—RMM

Contents

Acknowledgments

I have to first thank my mom and dad, Sharon and Robert Munroe. Without their love, support, international money wire transfers, and 2 a.m. emergency pep talks (long distance—charges reversed) I would still be writing sophomoric (semi-plagiarized from Norman Mailer) drivel in a welfare hotel room in some random Canadian city. You two are the best!

Big thanks to the rest of my biological and adopted family for being such wonderful supporters of my work—Davie, Miguel, Sergio, Billy, Nicola, Rykie, Serena, Blair, Cory Richard, Phil, Roberta Marlene, and Wilma and Joe. Thank you to my hubby, Basil Tsiokos, for convincing me to see the undeniable value of my Americanization. And of course, to my second mom, J.S., who long, long ago, taught me the value of being able to tell a good story.

Thank you to Romaine Clifton, my Platonic match made in heaven, who for two years listened, advised, and was a loving witness to the development of my creativity.

Kudos to my uber talented and *very* patient editor, Mr. Brendan Duffy, and to his predecessor, Zareen Jaffrey, who from the start supported this book wholeheartedly. Thanks to all the staff at Hyperion Books who have made this process a great one, especially their amazing editor in chief, Mr. Will Balliet.

Thank you, Meaghan Nanson, for transcribing a ridiculous

number of hours of interviews—I'd *still* be listening to those recordings if it wasn't for you. Huge thanks to Steven Tagle for copious research and late-night color corrections. Thank you, Tom Quinn, for the brilliant foreword!

Thank you to all the filmmakers (from directors to post-production colleagues), to the film executives, programmers, and actors who responded to requests for interviews, quotes, and last-minute addendums. While I may have not used all (or any) of what you shared, your contribution to this book was invaluable.

Grand thanks to John Cooper, Geoffrey Gilmore, Shari Frilot, Trevor Groth, and the rest of the crew at Sundance for imparting your wisdom for more than five years. And a special thanks to Mike Plante for four years, 16,000 submissions, 22,347 emails, 13,453 phone calls, 376 chocolate-covered pretzels, and hundreds of hours sharing in the joy of hand-painted film and asynchronous sound.

A million thank yous to Orly Ravid for not only treating me like a mutual fund as I wrote this book, but for being such a beautiful friend and inspirational writing companion. On behalf of Marcello and myself, we are forever indebted to Jennifer Nashorn and Joshua Blankenship for not only being great friends and book supporters, but also for being the best godparents a Min-Pin could ask for. Deep appreciation to my students at Inner-City Filmmakers for reminding me that truly great filmmaking really is all about teamwork.

Thank you to my dear friends Michaline Babich (say it ten times fast) and Tiffany Shlain. You were the first filmmakers to say, "Roberta, you need to write a book, and *we're going to help you*." I know that without morning coffee in Mill Valley and writing extravaganzas in Nichols Canyon (Thank you, Ellen!) I may very well have thrown in the towel. Thank you to Danielle Lurie and Joshua Leonard for our *Mutual Admiration Club* coffee klatches in Echo Park—where much of this book's essence was born.

I'll admit, I get a little teary-eyed when I get to thanking the three people for whom the *finishing* (really, anyone can *start* writing a book) of this book would not have been possible.

To my sister Diana I say simply, *you are outstanding.* With your love and care I am guaranteed to be the person I always dreamed of being. Thank you for being there every step of the way. It is without hyperbole that I say I couldn't have done it without you.

To my dear friend and fellow writer, Dennis H. T. Ruud. Thank you for cross-country movie-making road trips, winter nights in Alberta playing Scrabble, writing retreats in Kingman, Arizona, and for being relentless in your support of this endeavour and your love for me.

And finally, a world of gratitude to my agent, Jason Anthony, at Lippincott Massie McQuilkin—the only person who has read this book as many times as I have. Thank you for gently (and not so gently) pushing me through the proposal and revision process. All CIM jokes aside, this book could not and *would not* have happened without your constant support and expertise. Jason, it is with all my heart I say thank you. For everything.

Foreword

In a business that's littered with financial ruin, consumed by naïve expectations, fueled by fragile egos, and beleaguered by a hundred-year-old system designed to keep the uncompromising and unconnected artist out of the mainstream, one has to wonder: Why the hell would any sane individual want to direct a feature film . . . *ever*? Even the 2% of the 2% of working directors who secure distribution and "make it," with the requisite awards and financial success, there's still much heartache, frustration, and countless sleepless nights that go along with it. Even good marriages go bad. It's a rat race of epic proportions where only the blood-drunk with ambition survive. Yikes.

Now take those friendly odds, cut them by 99.9%, and you've rolled the dice on your future career as a short filmmaker. That's assuming of course that you've mastered the fine art of making a short film, which in many ways trumps making a full-length feature. Mark Twain was famous for writing succinctly, but even he lamented the trials and tribulations of writing the short story: "It probably costs you nothing to write a short story but I find that it costs me as many false starts—and therefore failures—as does a long one." Clearly Twain never made a short film though, because while we've all heard about the democratization of film production, the distribution world still hasn't delivered a consistent model in which filmmakers could ever hope to recoup 20%

of the original investment in *best-case scenario*. Cheap it ain't. And financial successes like *Wallace & Gromit* or *George Lucas in Love* only come along once in a blue moon.

So why even bother? Right? Just throw in the towel, put this book down immediately, and go back to your temp McJob, your safe, uninspired, philistine cocoon, fall in love, start a family, and maybe pass away the weekends writing the great American short story. Right? Wrong! You've already demonstrated a few character traits most directors seem to lack:

1. A willingness to listen.
2. An attempt at practicality.
3. You're not relying on chutzpah alone.

While none of those things may be true (and that's okay), at least after having read this book you'll consider trying all three when making your short film.

There was a time not too long ago in the hyperridiculous dot-com era when every online hub and its corporate parent threw wads of cash at short filmmakers. The world had experienced streaming and the race was on for whoever could aggregate the most content and build a library. The Internet became an incubator for new talent run by big Hollywood luring droves of people (especially as they worked their nine-to-fives, driving ad sales, and building a fierce online community). Big companies like BMW and Chrysler got in on the craze too, making their own short films. Sundance threw some of the biggest parties I've ever seen borne on these potent little shorts. We were in the bubble and the future looked bright. Great filmmakers like David Birdsell, Mike Mitchell (*Herd,* my favorite short of all time, and good enough to forgive his movie *Deuce Bigalow: Male Gigolo*), and Mark Osborne (*More* has inspired so many imitations) were all riding high. And then we woke up. Everybody realized streaming blew (I still have nightmares about my dial-up tone) and the venture-capital dough vanished. We'd experienced a major depression in the shorts world before, though. In the era of the matinee idol, the American public had grown accustomed to seeing theatrical shorts where they were meant to be seen. And then Reagan got into office and it all went to sh*t. Okay, I have no clue why the theatrical short went away, but once again short filmmakers were an overlooked group relegated to an artistic ghetto: the animated and live-action shorts branch of the Academy chock full of prestigious awards given to films the paying public had never seen. If a tree falls in the forest and nobody . . . you get the tragedy here.

Well, like any good film executive, I'm about to contradict myself. The good news is that it's a new era for the short film and the future is looking brighter than ever. We're back in the bubble, but this go-around it's not just built on hype. The Academy-nominated shorts (all of them, including the documentary shorts) are being distributed across multiple platforms, including those old dinosaurs, movie theaters. This past year Magnolia Pictures (where I'm fortunate enough to earn a living), in conjunction with Shorts International, launched each animated and live-action short nominee theatrically, on DVD, and iTunes for the third year in a row. Prior to the awards show, just like any other nominated full-length feature. Finally, some respect. This year we grossed over $500K domestically. That might not sound like much, but if you consider that it places the series among the top half of *all* films released in any given year, it's an amazing feat—and that's with a very efficient marketing spend to boot.

And then there's YouTube. The behemoth juggernaut that's changing it all. If it weren't for YouTube I would have never seen that monkey drinking his urine, or Justin Timberlake wax poetic in *Dick in a Box* (best piece of entertainment regardless of running time in 2007), and some of our own illegally down-loaded Magnolia movies. If you're worried about people pirating your short online, then the only real protection afforded to any filmmaker is making a terrible film. Nobody will care. I promise. Otherwise there's nothing you can do. Consumers want good content and they want it immediately. Sometimes they're lazy too, though, and willing to pay if it's easy and affordable. Which begs the question: How the heck are we going to monetize You-Tube? I don't have the answer to that, but I love what it enables consumers to do. It's easy to use, like a free jukebox. It's got all your favorite songs, and once you find a favorite song you can't wait to share it with a buddy and play it for the whole bar. It builds a community based on short form content and teaches a whole generation how to enjoy and share it. Too bad you can't share that moment together in person, though. Seriously, how fantastic would it be seeing *Dick in a Box* at your local multi-plex with five hundred howling people. An experience I'm sure would rank up there with seeing the *South Park* movie at Grau-man's Chinese. Incidentally, the French are one step ahead of us. Two years ago a beautiful Oscar-short-listed animated short named *Imago* (approximately 15 minutes in length) was released theatrically as a stand-alone piece of entertainment. Who said a full-length feature had to be 82 minutes long?

Another incredible new platform for shorts is iTunes. You're not currently going to get rich distributing via iTunes, but as multiple territories open up around the world (UK and Australia having recently launched), the possibilities are limitless. I see an era where 100K units across the globe for a decent short is easy. It's by far the sexiest online store, so why not? And while the iPod may be too small for subtitles, it's still a great way to pass the time on your way to work, assuming of course you're not driving.

Shorts used to be merely calling cards for wannabe feature directors? Well, they're still calling cards, but they've also become first seed in developing feature-length content based on the same material. Some of my favorite examples: *Five Feet High and Rising* became *Raising Victor Vargas; Cashback* became *Cashback*.

So the world is opening up in a way that may have lasting effects for the short filmmaker. You still have to make a good film though, because content is king and will always be king. If you can't nail that execution-dependent "secret sauce" quality of what makes a film good, then I guess go back to writing that great American short story instead. While no expert can ever know anything truly (this industry is like a golf swing; the more you know, the less you know), Roberta herein is the only writer who's ever addressed what not to do creatively, what to do practically, and how to execute it. So read the book and go make a short that just might find its way into the Sundance catalog.

Oh, and please send it to me when you're done. I'd love to get a jump on this year's Oscar nominees.

Break a leg.

Tom Quinn
Magnolia Pictures

Introduction

My name is Roberta Munroe and it has been said on many an occasion that I know more about short film than anyone else in the world. Not true. But, I have watched over 15,000 short films, helped hundreds of short filmmakers realize their dreams, and made my own award-winning short films, *Dani and Alice,* and now *Happy Birthday.*

Nevertheless, there are people out there who say, "Who the hell is Roberta Munroe and why should I listen to her?" Then there's the old, "Screw Roberta Munroe, I'm making my film 43 minutes long, with my handheld home video camera, I'm hiring my barely talented girlfriend to play the lead, AND I'm going to edit it myself!"

Right.

Why not just say, "I could care less if my film gets programmed at any festival, never mind Sundance." Or perhaps you could say, "I'm too afraid to be successful so I'll just continue to make these rotten short films and complain to my friends when the rejection letters pour in."

It's also been said on more than one occasion that you have to *know or have sex* with me (or one of my former colleagues) to get your film in Sundance (or Clermont-Ferrand, Cinematexas— pull out your last rejection letter and fill in the blank). These same people also say that submissions are only watched by volunteer or lowly paid screeners and if these purportedly moronic peons don't like it, your film won't get passed on to a "real" programmer and therefore never see the light of day.

That's nonsense. We watched everything—yep, even yours. And every other film festival's programmers are acting with the same integrity. No one wants to miss that next great film just because they're exhausted. It's a film programmer's life's mission to find the best of the best. Seriously.

There are thousands of short films traveling the festival circuits, and it's a programmer's job to wade through them. Seems like a lot of work? Well, it is. Let me put it into perspective for you. When I first began putting together the short program at Sundance we received around 2,200 short films and we watched every one submitted.

That was 2001 and we selected about 90 shorts. By 2006 we received 4,532—more than double the number in 2001—and the selected number *dropped* to 85. As of 2008, the submitted number of shorts was 5,400, and once again the number of selected films dropped, to 84. *That means less than 2% of the shorts submitted were selected.* Which is why your film needs to be great. And, believe me, it can be.

WHY MAKE A SHORT FILM?

Why would one make a short? The most popular reason is to create a calling card to shop around to agents, managers, and distributors. Some filmmakers believe that if you can show your talents in 15 minutes you can find someone (like an agent) to find you feature film or television work.

But let's look at the numbers.

At any given time, there are roughly 10,000 directors with a short film under their arms shopping it around to the perhaps

500 legit agents and managers. You need to know how to make yours stand out from the masses.

Then there are the people for whom short format work is a stand-alone artistic endeavor. Generally speaking, these filmmakers create visual art that is meant to appear with other creative work (e.g., spoken word). Confident that this work will garner them a career, these artists hope to be courted by museums, art shows, and galleries. Curators seek out this work at film festivals, self-designed installation art shows, as well as through submissions. And then there is that rare breed of short filmmaker who has no desire to be a writer/director but instead plans to produce. Their foray into the short filmmaking world is solely for the experience.

Most filmmakers make a short film before they go on to longer-form projects. The first time they sit down to write, they may write a feature-length script but, with few exceptions, filmmakers first practice their craft in the short-format genre.

And of course there are the "No, I'm not a filmmaker, I just like to make little movies on my computer for fun" types—like my friend Dennis Ruud, a brilliant writer, who is always around with his digital camera positioned on "video" at every family gathering. There's plenty of useful information in this book for you too!

You probably first picked up this book because a five-year Sundance shorts programmer wrote it. This book is my not-so-humble opinion as well as those of over twenty truly gifted filmmakers and several seasoned industry folk maximized over 200 or so pages.

So many films are well-written, well-structured, with medium-to-good performances and pretty good length, but ultimately fail because of one reason—the director didn't listen. She didn't listen to herself, to her producer who has already done this ten times, to the actor who couldn't get the words to tumble out of his mouth and needed a script revision, or to the script supervisor* who insisted that the close-up and master didn't match.

Or worse, the director *did* listen a little too closely to the director of photography, who thought he was shooting *Master and Commander*, to the producer who is working on seven other projects and barely remembers what your story is about, to the actor who feels as though your warmhearted protagonist would play better as a more De Niro version of Tony Soprano, and to the script supervisor who has been texting her girlfriend all morning.

WHY ARE SO FEW FILMS GOOD?

It's somewhat difficult to explain what makes a successful short film, but there are certainly crystal clear ways to explain what makes an unsuccessful short film, and we'll expand on the reasons below in later chapters.

- Length does not match story—it's too short or too long.
- Self-indulgent.
- Poorly cast.
- Poorly written.
- Self-edited and not enough fat cut out.
- Not enough research done.
- Not a short film but obviously a scene from a feature.
- Hi, it's called a tripod.
- Your best friend is not a cinematographer.
- Your girlfriend is not an actress.
- Your Holocaust surviving grandmother, while amazing, is not that interesting to the general population when you compress her greatness into her poorly lit kitchen.

---

* See Chapter 5 for crew descriptions.

- Though breast cancer affects us all, home-video-edited films don't always make for good short films.
- You and your friends' road trip to Vegas is not a movie.
- All Black men are not drug dealers and/or pimps.
- You can't just throw money at something to make it better—you and your rich parents don't make you a filmmaker.

Like your film should be, this book is going to be relatively short and to the point. There are a few *How to Make a Short Film* books out there. However, I have challenged myself and enlisted the help of some truly great people to write a book that actually tells you not only how to increase the odds of making a great short but also *How NOT to Make a Rotten, Unwatchable, Unprogrammable Short Film*. I know you can make a great film—it's only a matter of having the resources to do so. All of the filmmakers in this book share their successes and their failures. Pay close attention.

As you may have figured out by now, this book is not for the easily disenchanted. Filmmaking is a tough business, and you need to be a little tough too. You and your sad-sack stories are going to get the slap-down. Prepare yourself.

But if you stick around you will learn:

- The top clichés that plague the short filmmaker.
- How to create a worthwhile story.
- Casting and location tips.
- What a short film producer does and doesn't do.
- Inside information on what Sundance and other top-tier festivals are looking for.
- YouTube, iTunes, Revver, and other new media short film platforms.
- What successful filmmakers believe are the tricks of the short filmmaking trade.

- What programmers are *really* saying when they watch your film.
- Editing do's and don'ts.
- The laws of post-production.
- Distribution—yes, with a little work, you can have it all!
- And, yes, taking home video movies counts as film-making.

Filmmaking is a business. Filmmaking is an art. Filmmaking can be done on film, on video, or on your laptop. Filmmaking can be something you see as your career, or a way to capture memories on your handheld digital recorder of your children, which you can then make them (and their children) sit through thirty years down the road. Filmmaking can be live action with or without dialogue, Claymation, hand-drawn animation, computer generated, or stop motion, or a combination of all of the above. Yes, I agree (along with a hundred million other users) that you can make an interesting, watchable film on your cellular phone or digital camera.

However, there are rules for every format. Your romantic comedy set in broad daylight may require film rather than the harsh realities of video (and sometimes the other way around) and may fall flat if shot on your phone (while your surreal and lyrical experimental piece might work fine shot on your Motorola). We'll go further in depth with this in the Crewing Up chapter, where we'll talk about the different kinds of directors of photography and media you may want to investigate.

Maybe you've been to film festivals locally, domestically, even internationally. You've watched short film after short film and often thought to yourself, I could do that! Well, of course you can. Thousands are already doing it. But I guarantee you that 80% of what is being made out there will make a film festival programmer's (and an audience's, or an agent's, or your mom's) eyes roll into the back of her head. Why? Because most budding filmmakers don't understand the structure of short filmmaking.

And believe me, there is a structure to the story, the script, the casting and crewing up, the length, and the post-production of your film. This is not only true for films that go on to festivals or make it onto television but also for the do-it-yourself type who, camera in hand, red light flashing, drives his family and friends running for the kitchen broom closet at every family bbq. You'll learn that, yes, even your dad can make lasting *and* entertaining short films of *your* family.

The following chapters will help you keep from falling into the traps of insipid filmmaking that have thwarted so many filmmakers before you. I'll share interviews with several very successful filmmakers and producers who have already braved the firewalk of short filmmaking. I also took notes during the many consulting sessions I've done with clients who were preparing for their first filmmaking experience. Though I tried to include ample information alongside their names, please be sure to go on IMDb to find out more. It's also important to note that in Chapter 5, "Crewing Up," there's a description of crew postions that you can refer to throughout the earlier chapters.

And, finally, after reading this book, what you'll learn is that if you really want to understand the intricacies of creating a really good short film—make one.

HOW **NOT** TO MAKE A SHORT FILM

Keep It Fresh
(Script Story)

```
         INT. WRITER'S OFFICE—DAY
An older white man with a beard sits at his
manual typewriter. He begins a story about
an artist living in the eighteenth century.
The artist finds himself in love with the
wrong woman, who finally betrays him by
killing him in his sleep. The writer types
away until he realizes that he has entered
his own story and this woman is now (sur-
prise) in his office seducing him with her
eyes and low-cut dress. The writer falls for
her as did his character. [And guess what?]
She kills the writer.
```

What?

The stakes are never higher than with the script. Don't make the mistake that many novice filmmakers do, which is to ignore story in favor of shooting a bunch of big Hollywood production value shots, stringing them together, and calling it a film.

I have to assume that if you're reading this book you already have an idea of the story you'd like to shoot. Perhaps your original idea will change after reading this book. Regardless, what you have to do is make sure this script is good enough to shoot, the length matches your story, AND that your story is a short one.

A great short begins with a solid story and characters. You need to know who these people are, what they look like, what kind of underwear they wear, what you'd like to happen to them, and most importantly, what they want and what *they'd* like to happen to them. Yes, you should make sure the wardrobe matches the character—often a simple outfit tells us who this character is in that first ten seconds we meet them. As does the job they do, the person they're sleeping with (or not sleeping with), the language they use, and the breakfast drink they choose. People are not stupid. If your character walks out of his bedroom in boxer shorts and ratty Rolling Stones T-shirt, makes coffee, and lights up a cigarette, an audience member in Nigeria will understand the essence of this setup. (But remember, if I just used that as an example it means I've seen it a hundred times and you should seek out a fresher way to *show* the "Guy with a Dream but No Willpower to Achieve It" character.) When you *know* your characters you'll understand exactly how to get "who they are" across to the audience.

HOW TO LOSE YOUR PROGRAMMER/AUDIENCE FROM SCENE ONE

Over the years I have watched more films than I (and my colleagues) care to remember with the following story lines:

The Tragic Buddy Film

Two soldiers (pick a war—Iraq, Vietnam, WWII, WWI—I've seen them all) struggle through the snow/rain/mud/forest/desert. One is wounded/angry/desperate and the other is proud/quiet/rebellious. There are flashbacks to battle, letters or pictures of girlfriends pulled out of pockets, and they usually run out of water/food and end up barely escaping the enemy by hiding out in some dirt hole or farm basement. Or, worse, they are each from opposite armies (British vs. Italian, German vs. American, etc.) and have to help each other stay alive. Whatever.

The Latino Drug Lord/Black Gangster Film

I put these together because they are essentially the same film (sometimes it's the Irish Good Old Boys with Guns film). I've seen this film several hundred times and from the opening sequence I know exactly what's going to happen—and, my friend, so do all of my colleagues.

Two guys, one a "good-looking natural-born killer," the other his "not-so-committed-to-the-cause, not-that-great-looking best friend." They either steal money/drugs from other criminals, find a bunch of money that belongs to other criminals, or they *are* the avenging criminals trying to get their drugs/money back. The twist on this one is when the "not-so-committed-to-the-cause best friend" is the "little brother who is about to graduate from high school but gets shot by accident instead." The Hughes Brothers have moved on—so should you.

The Poetic/Lyrical Non-Linear Ode to Ex-Girlfriend

Plenty of old photos, Coldplay (unlicensed of course) underscores the entire film, shots of the ocean, steel-gray skies, a laughing couple playfully wrestling in the sun at Griffith Park, maybe even eating cotton candy at Coney Island. CUT TO: lonely guy or girl watching TV alone, walking along wetted down streets smoking, wandering aimlessly in and out of all the old favorite places they used to go.

Do what the rest of us do when we have a hard breakup. Write bleak poetry (that you show no one), compose raging e-mails (saved as a draft and never sent), find a good therapist, and call Tony Robbins.

The *Cold Mountain* Film

This is the period-piece film. There are the slave woman and man tucked away in their beds conspiring about their imminent escape. Or it's the Black slave woman who is in love with the white master (or the other way around, or it's the white woman and her *Mandingo*). Could be about Jesus Christ, could be about the Apache slave trade. Doesn't matter—they don't work.

It's extremely difficult to nail a period piece with millions of dollars (just ask the producers of *Alexander* or *Marie Antoinette*). So your film shot in the park by your house, the Palm Springs desert, or beneath the Brooklyn Bridge is set up to fail . . . miserably. I remember programming just one short with this setup. It was *Red Mud* (*Rosso Fango*, Italy) and it had a huge budget (over $50,000), was an international selection with government financial backing, was shot on 35mm, and had a very slick twist.

I am also reminded of *The Last King of Scotland*. Forest Whitaker and James McAvoy are brilliant actors; the script is great and based on a true story. The film was shot in Africa and the UK, where the story takes place. Slowly, over 121 minutes, the character of Idi Amin is revealed. The filmmaker and producers had access to shoot in Uganda, had the means to re-create an entire era and had true professionals working in production design, research and wardrobe. And *still* there are no less than twelve sightings of factual and anachronistic errors in the film listed on IMDb. Millions of dollars and countless top-notch professionals later, there were errors. Do you really think your $12,000-budgeted WWII short is up for the challenge?

The Prostitute (Homeless Man, Curmudgeon Who Lives Next Door) With a Heart of Gold Film

A fairly drab housewife who hates her kids, her husband, her job, her colleagues, and ultimately herself meets up with one of the above. Sometimes it's a man with the same storyline only he has already lost his wife, kids, job, and will to live. Along comes a prostitute, or a homeless man, or the nosy old lady next door who teaches them how to be grateful for what he or she has. After a four-minute conversation, the woman becomes the dream mom, wife, mother, and employee or the man gets his wife, kids, job, and self-esteem back.

Okay, for one thing, if and when this does happen in real life, it is only interesting to the person it happens to (save a few buddies at the neighborhood bar who listen "politely" to this life-changing moment). Unless, of course, I'm watching *Oprah*. And if I am, it's *why* I'm watching *Oprah*. I want to see the *real* people telling their *real* stories. If you really feel the need to make this kind of film—make a documentary (but first read the section below on documentaries).

The Dream/Suicide Film

This is possibly one of the most excruciating short film ideas *ever*. Your protagonist is dead and he doesn't know it; is contemplating suicide but her daughter runs into the room with her report card so the lead drops the pill bottle behind the couch; OR, worse, the protagonist dies a horrible death only for the audience to be "shocked" by the fact that it was all a dream. But the ultimate worst story idea in this genre is when the lead kills someone accidentally (usually a child while he's driving drunk or angry), is *then* killed accidentally by the ghost of the dead child, and the two live in some sort of experimentally shot purgatory forever. I've seen this film way too many times and it rarely hits its mark. Stop yourself.

The Rip-off Film

Oddball guy, gets pushed around at school, laments over not having a chance with the popular girl, has an even more oddball best friend (male or female, usually overweight and smokes) who encourages him to try out for the football (baseball, chess, polo) team to get the girl's attention. Coach is a madman megalomaniac who brings him on only to see him get his legs broken, his mom drinks vodka in her morning coffee and smokes in the broom closet while his dad polishes his guns, teaches English literature at the local college, and tells his son he's a moron every chance he gets. Guy gets winning goal (home run, checkmate, whatever), gets the girl, and learns to tango. WTF?

Let me make one last plea. In the five years I was at Sundance I think we showed maybe three or four narrative shorts that included one of the above storylines—*in five years*. You're already working with a less than 2% chance of getting into top-tier fests—don't further lessen your chances by copying someone else's work.

Seasoned producer Vanessa Coifman, Executive Vice President of Production and Development at Senator Entertainment, who produced, among many other films, *Fireflies in the Garden*, which premiered at the 2008 Berlinale International Film Festival (starring Ryan Reynolds, Emily Watson, Willem Dafoe, and Julia Roberts) took a few moments out of her hectic schedule to give her take on this. Vanessa clearly outlines the deal with the devil you want to avoid:

"[A rip-off of someone else's work] is obvious immediately. You *know* when somebody's trying to be something that they're not. And if you can mimic them, there's probably work for you out there, but it'll never be something that you want to do. You'll become a director for hire, for people who want a film to *look* like Wes Anderson. You're going to fall into a hole that you're never going to be able to step out of. You *must* start with your own voice."

My friend, believe me when I tell you it is painfully obvious that you have watched *Napoleon Dynamite, Reservoir Dogs, Steel Magnolias, Saving Private Ryan, Requiem for a Dream, The Royal Tenenbaums, The Color Purple,* or *Schindler's List* twenty times. Guess what they were? Feature films. Guess what you can't make them into? Short films. Guess what neither programmers nor audience members want to see? A scene, entirely out of context, that is a rip-off of one of these films. Don't do it.

The Cancer/Crack Addict Parent/Holocaust Documentary

All of a sudden during lunch one Friday afternoon, Bubbe starts telling you the story of her escape from Europe during Hitler's terrorizing reign. You run, grab your camera, and voilà, you have a compelling documentary about the Holocaust.

No, no, you don't. You have your grandmother telling her incredibly poignant story beside an open window (with traffic and pedestrian noise intermittently drowning out her voice), lit with a 60-watt light bulb (making her look like she's auditioning for *Dawn of the Dead IV*), and of course the light bulb is flickering—which is *impossible* to fix in post, where she forgets she's on camera and often walks out of frame to get more tea or talk to your aunt Ruth in the other room (who has forbidden you from turning the camera on her).

Or you find out that you have cancer and want to document your journey. Or you learn that the women of the neighborhood are losing their Community Garden to the greedy corporation that owns the property and won't sell it to them. Or you run into some crack addicts living on skid row who allow you to follow them around while they get high.

I'm not going to be flippant about these documentary stories, but I am going to be honest. If it is unbelievably difficult to make a good narrative short film, it can be said that it is just this side of impossible to make a *compelling* documentary short film. Yes, Bubbe is an incredible woman who raised your mom perfectly, who in turn was able to raise you well. Yes, going through radiation and chemotherapy is undeniably difficult and your journey will inspire all those around you. Yes, crack (meth, cocaine, alcohol) addiction is ruining lives worldwide. Just know that these topics affect millions of people, which means there are hundreds (if not *thousands*) of filmmakers making these documentaries—so yours better be beyond compelling. It better be heart-stopping and breathtaking.

Do an online search for Jonna Tamases' *Jonna's Body,* Cynthia Wade's Oscar-winning *Freeheld,* Selena A. Burks' *Saving Jackie,* Hanna Polak's *Children of Leningradsky* and Gina Levy and Eric Johnson's *Foo-Foo Dust.* These are just a few of the powerful short documentaries I have seen that cover familiar territory with spectacular results. Once you start searching, I guarantee that you will find many great films that will put into perspective what a truly great documentary short can accomplish.

With docs, you tend to have a lot more leeway than narrative, experimental, or animated short films in terms of running time. The audience is required to become emotionally invested in *real* people, saying *real* things. This takes time. Sure, I've seen lovely docs that are four minutes long; however, their subjects, their stories' purpose only needed four minutes to be revealed and are often far lighter in tone than most documentaries.

As both a programmer and an audience member it is difficult for me to decide when a doc sucks. This is someone's real life up there on that screen—who am I to judge? Well, what I've learned along the way is that I'm not judging the subjects themselves; I'm judging your ability to reveal them in a cinematic, honorable, and honest way. First, you need to deeply explore what and whom you have chosen to document and then—*most importantly*—be able to *show* us, your audience, why you've chosen them.

I spoke with Diane Weyermann, one of the few people in this industry I consider a mentor. Diane has been a supporter of documentary storytelling since her early work at Open Society Institute and the Soros Foundation. She was also instrumental in the development of the Sundance Documentary Fund. Over the course of her career, Diane was involved with the production of over three hundred documentaries around the world. Her present position is Executive Vice President in charge of Documentary Production at Participant Media (www.partici pantmedia.com). Participant has executive produced or coproduced several extraordinary works, including *An Inconvenient Truth, Darfur Now, Film, Inc.*, and the narrative films *Charlie Wilson's War* and *The Visitor*. Diane took a few moments out of her hectic schedule to talk with me, and she shares:

> "Sometimes the most universal stories are those small stories. It doesn't have to be a big massive issue-related story, it can be small as long as it has that larger resonance. I would say that there are a lot of personal stories out there that may not work as films because they are simply too personal, too myopic. If you want to tell a family story, that story has to transcend your specific family relationships. I would also say you have to look at the body of work that exists and as [Roberta] indicated there are many *many* films about a grandmother who survived the Holocaust. What makes this film different? What are you bringing to the subject that we haven't yet seen?"

When writing the treatment for your documentary ask yourself repeatedly, page by page: *What am I bringing to this subject that we haven't yet seen?*

And the documentary conundrum of what to shoot and when to turn the camera off is a huge one. You may have a storyline in mind, but during the shoot things could shift dramatically due to an unexpected moment.

When I spoke with director of photography Alison Kelly, we were able to talk about the backstory of a documentary that she'd shot. It was clear to me that she'd turned off the camera to protect one of the subjects, who was under the influence of alcohol. I asked her how she deals with the dichotomy of having a job to do and having morals and personal integrity to uphold. She explains:

> "I think you have to use yourself as a guide. There are people that I have worked with that have a really different threshold for what is appropriate, and I think there are people who are much more motivated by what they see in a situation as the potential for commercial success of their indie documentary—by the same token, if the subject is okay with that, I'm not going to judge them for being okay with it. I just know that if it were me, I would have felt like a total asshole if I let that go down. But I've certainly come across people in the film business that not only would have let it go down, but have instigated the situation to make it more dramatic. I think people are so conditioned to feel okay with invading people's space and lives. We see it on TV all the time. The key thing for me, in doing a doc, is that you need to (even more so than with narrative work) be able to trust the team of people you're going in with. Because you're going into a real situation, into real people's lives, and if you don't feel these are people that you share a common respect for space and other people's lives, then you shouldn't be doing it. I've actually turned down jobs because I knew I would be put in a situation where I would feel like I'd have to turn the camera off and leave the room, just because of the way the person was handling the whole thing—why

put yourself through it? I would say the most important thing is just to trust your gut. Every time I haven't trusted my gut I've regretted it. I've been in a lot of people's homes and lives, and particularly as a doc shooter, you get looked at, as the one holding the camera, as the one who has the control. But in reality the entire crew is the team and if you have someone on your team that is just generally not a decent person, it's the shittiest feeling because they [the subjects] look at you as a team. And that one weak link can bring the whole team down."

Experimental

Story and structure are equally as important in experimental filmmaking as they are in live-action narratives and straightforward documentaries. The main difference between narrative and experimental is that experimental films are often more poetic than dialogue driven, have certain aspects of filmmaking that are outside the mainstream box (repetitive editing, non-linear storytelling, lengthy shots with minimal movement or action), and most notably, an emphasis on sound design.

I learned a lot from Mike Plante (one of the programmers of Sundance's experimental section, the New Frontier) over our four years together at Sundance programming shorts. You *have* to check out Mike's Web site, www.iblamesociety.com. During this eye-opening time, experimental filmmaking became one of my favorite genres. So much creativity (and time!) is put into successful experimental works it's awe-inspiring.

I also learned while following experimental filmmakers' careers that most of them are working with the tiniest of budgets that are self-financed, or financed through small grants, and that you're working with a minimal crew or oftentimes alone. It just cannot be easy to go up to your family and say, "I want to make a 15-minute short film of tugboats crossing the bay. Will you give me $3,000?"

But if the insertion of experimental work in mainstream media is any indication of times to come, I think doing this might get a little easier—because it's *everywhere*. Once you start looking, you see it in mainstream filmmaking, commercials, Web site marketing—that out-of-focus look, the painting or scratching on film look, the non-linear rapid editing and the use of asynchronous sound work.

Some remarkable filmmakers who have incorporated their experimental sensibilities in their feature filmmaking are Kathryn Bigelow, Isaac Julien, Gus Van Sant, Susan Friedman, Chantal Ackerman, and Peter Greenaway.

Experimental work within mainstream filmmaking happens often without the audience ever knowing what the impetus was for certain spellbinding shots or editing techniques. *Se7en* (which stars Morgan Freeman and Brad Pitt) owes a huge amount of thanks to Stan Brakhage (a prolific experimental filmmaker and professor) for its outstanding opening credit sequence. Who knew?

Mike Plante remarks:

"You'd be surprised how much story and emotion you can get from something experimental—a flawed term since those films are much more planned than experiments, but it *is* a catchy word. If you go to film fests around the country that show truly diverse work, then you start to realize that underground and unusual film work is everywhere, people working from their bedrooms separate from the mainstream world but, in a way, together."

Shirin Neshat—*Turbulent* (1998), *Rapture* (1999), *Fervor* (2000), *Soliloquy* (1999), *Possessed* (2001), *Pulse* (2001), *Passage* (2001), and *Tooba* (2002)—is an award-winning artist, filmmaker, and author whose works have been featured at some of the most prestigious galleries and festivals all over the world. Shirin shares:

"I'm not sure if it's an experimental filmmaker's responsibility to educate the mainstream audience because really a film-maker's task is simply to *make* his or her film however experimental that might be. There seems to be always an audience for such films, even if it's a small one. Having said that, while making my films, I constantly had to ask myself and others, whether a certain meaning of the film was transparent or not. Through the various test screenings, I was surprised how often many, including non-mainstream audience, missed some of the most significant aspects of the narrative. This of course was very helpful for me to go back to the editing table and consider the problem. So at the end, you as a filmmaker hope to make a film that maintains the right balance in between being accessible to the public while remaining somewhat enigmatic."

Yes, the use of various abstracting techniques can be exquisitely beautiful and thought-provoking and depending on your goals they can even bring in the dollars—but if your work looks like all you did was copy Stan Brakhage's work you're in trouble. Considering he was one of the most important American filmmakers of the twentieth century, yes, you should be studying his work. But just make sure yours isn't anything one would consider an exact copy.

I know it doesn't seem as easy to research experimental work as it is linear narrative or documentary; however, Canyon Cinema in San Francisco has a great Web site and is the distributor of more than 3,500 experimental works including those of Stan Brakhage (www.canyoncinema.com). Do your research.

ANIMATION

As you'll learn later, in Chapter 10, I have an undeniable emotional attachment to animation. All those Saturday mornings spent as a child watching Looney Tunes or imagining myself to be Wonder Woman could be the cause, but I think, in all serious-ness, what really captivates me is the sheer genius and ridiculous amount of time and creativity it takes to create great animation. As with experimental work, I am awed by its impact.

However, like all artistic work, unoriginal storylines or technique can befall the animator. I reached out to Chris Robinson, the Artistic Director of the Ottawa International Animation Festival. One of the largest animation festivals in the world, the OIAF receives over 2,000 submissions every year and they program somewhere around 150. Chris shares his views with us:

> "First off, and maybe I'll be ostracized for this, but anima-tors are way more down to earth than the majority of live-action filmmakers I've met. Some of it is a confidence thing. Animators, at least the indies, are working *directly* with their art. They're often alone. So, they're confident about who they are and what they're doing. Their film, good or bad, is *their* film. I wish that more animators who submit to Ottawa actually went to the festival first (and if not Ottawa, then they should go to some of the other respected animation festivals). Seeing the work and meeting other art-ists of your ilk—especially in such a marginalized art form as animation—is absolutely essential.
>
> "Also, while it is changing to some degree, there seems to be more of a satisfaction with making short works [within the animation filmmaking community]. In live ac-tion, the short film is generally just the stepping stone, the farm team along the way to the big league of features. In animation, short works are viewed as a legitimate art form—like the short story."

Hmm, maybe that's another reason I have such an affection for animation—it is quite comfortable in the short form genre without needing to aspire to feature length. From the 1-minute moments to epic 35-minute works, good animated films carry enough weight to satisfy at any length.

WRITE WHAT YOU KNOW

Some people will say otherwise, but I think you're on the wrong track if you don't choose a story that you have some personal connection to when you're directing your first film. If you don't, it will be tremendously difficult. Give yourself a break on your first kick at the can. There will be hundreds of things you need to worry about both on and off set, and it's important to have an intuitive grasp of the story so these other tasks get your best work. (And another reason to stick with what you know: A veteran programmer or an average audience member can *feel* when the filmmaker isn't realizing *his* vision but instead one that he thinks will garner the most attention. It's a sixth sense that film lovers and curators develop very quickly.)

Michaline Babich is a great filmmaker and television producer (*The Big O*, Feature Doc Competition Los Angeles Film Festival, 2001; *Kiss and Tell*, Short Doc Competition Sundance, 2003; *Million Dollar Listing*, on BRAVO; *Gimme Sugar*, on MTV's Logo 2008). In 2006, after several award-winning television documentary series, she decided to make her first narrative short. "Great," I said, "what's it about?" Gay. Male. Sex.

Now, the last time she'd had sex with a man (she has been a lesbian since birth) was in the last century and, as far as I know, she's never had sex with a gay man. Suffice it to say, she was a nervous wreck on set. She'd have all these great ideas, then was filled with anxiety as she turned to her actors to find out if they in fact would do whatever it was she was rewriting on the fly. It's only because she's a seasoned television supervising and executive producer and is used to bluffing that she was able to pull it off and not lose the confidence of her crew and actors.

Ultimately the film did very well on the festival circuit and in distribution, but when asked she says:

"You have enough things to worry about while directing your first film. Do something you know. So you can focus on the camera, on the actors, on the performance. Your crew and actors have to trust you. Make it easy on yourself. Trust me, it's going to be hard enough. During my shoot I was a prime candidate for Botox, Xanax addiction, *and* alcoholism."

HOW DO I KNOW THIS SCRIPT IS WORTH SHOOTING?

I'll admit something here. I *always* think my first draft is genius. Many of my friends think theirs are too. It's the nature of the beast. That's our job as artists—to believe in the art we create. However, the truth is I don't know a single filmmaker (including myself) who actually shot the first draft of their script. That first draft is there to act as a guideline for the genius you will eventually film. Now, there are several ways to get your script into shooting shape just by reaching out and contacting the right people.

Hire a Script Consultant

There are plenty of professional script consultants. The prices are generally affordable. A feature script consultant often garners between $350 and $500; with a short film script this price drops, to around $125 to $250. The benefits to having a professional read your script are obvious. They have read thousands of scripts and can offer a plethora of notes. They've read genre scripts, experimental, comedy, and documentary treatments time and time again. They know what is already out there being made and what you can do with your script to make it fresh. Investigate their client lists. Look for recent success stories on their Web sites. Contact filmmakers they've worked with. *Anyone* can call her- or himself a script consultant, but without client success stories/testimonials you may not get what you paid for.

But don't get all crazy on me. Sending your script to a paid consultant before it's finished could very well be a huge waste of money. In my consulting business, I'm sure I've had clients who wished they'd written more before sending their script to me only for me to tell them they needed to do a lot more work before I would be able to help them in any significant way. Wait until you've vetted the story thoroughly or make the decision that you're going to pay someone more than once to provide feedback. But if you've got a bunch of cash lying around for script development, I've had a few clients who simply sent a story outline for perusal. I sent back notes accordingly, then they wrote more and re-sent me the updated version when they needed a second round of feedback. Be very clear with yourself, your budget, your readers, and anyone you hire.

Friends: The Pros & Cons

Be careful about taking your draft and asking *friends* who have (or don't have) some writing experience to read it. Not only are most people not qualified to give you notes on your script, they also may be afraid to tell you the truth if it stinks.

But if you do have someone whom you are convinced will give you good, honest feedback, then do it. But the bottom line is you have to first identify what their strengths and perspectives are. For example, if you give me your script you should know that I have a strong bias against scripts with all white people where they could effortlessly be any race (and on the same note, where all the characters are male or female when they could be either), where people of color are background filler, stereotyped, or are stand-out tokens, scripts that include unnecessary rape scenes, and I hate scripts that have gay men talking like it's 1987 and the term *"Oh Mary, give it up"* is a fresh one. One friend might say, "It's perfect, don't change a thing," while another will say, "The characters are transparent and unevolved and the story is clichéd and stupid." Same script with totally different reads. You need to be able to process their feedback while not losing what it is you want to accomplish in your writing.

And the same is true when seeking rough-cut feedback. Documentary filmmaker Tiffany Shlain (*Life, Liberty, & The Pursuit of Happiness*, Sundance 2003; *The Tribe*, Sundance 2006; www.tif fanyshlain.com) recalls the moment after showing her rough cut to a group of filmmaker and non-filmmaker friends:

> "Often I'll show my work to a group of amazing advisors whose opinion I respect, people like, oh let's say Roberta Munroe [laughs]. These are people who will give me feedback that almost always changes the way I'm looking at the story, so much so that I go back to the edit and rethink my entire film. This is when feedback is at its best. But I've also had my share of devastating rough cut screenings where I invited a group over where they wrote down their feedback/critiques and just tore my film to pieces! I had spent *months* working on this cut and I was absolutely devastated by the feedback. So I said to one of them, 'Well, didn't you like *anything* about it??' And they were like, 'Oh my god, yes! I loved this, I loved that' and I asked, 'Why didn't you say any of that?' And it was all due to the way I asked for the feedback. What filmmakers need to know is that your average person thinks a 'critique' is what they didn't like. Make sure to go around the room and ask them to tell you a few things they did like—casting, pacing, music—before they move on to what they didn't like. We're all human beings, and these films are our babies after all. Learn how to ask for what you need."

Okay, maybe you live in a fishing village on the coast of Newfoundland and the closest thing you've got to a script reader is your aunt Betty. Hi, it's called the Internet. In the Resource Guide at the back of this book there are several online filmmaker communities listed. There is an extraordinary independent filmmaking community out there. Log on and tap into it.

Making a Film for Friends and Family

As technology continues to give us increasingly easier formats to create movies in, people are switching from photographs as keepsakes to digital home movies. This is a remarkable advance. Now, instead of albums of poorly lit, badly framed photographs that no one looks at after their initial viewing, people are able to make movies (!) of their vacations, family gatherings, and other special moments, throw them into a simple moviemaking program (software that's part of every new operating system whether it's Mac- or PC-based) and either spit out a DVD to mail or upload the film onto a Web site for relatives and friends around the world to view. As someone in love with the short film format, I am ecstatic about this development.

There really are ways to make a good home movie and ways not to. If you know Aunt Paula will talk for half an hour telling an old family story everyone has already heard a million times, *turn around* and find Aunt Judy, who will knock your socks off with all the family secrets she knows. It's easy (read safe) to approach the person who'll gab forever, but might be far more appealing and creative to actually film someone sharing your family's history that will come as a lovely surprise to everyone.

For example, my mother's sixtieth birthday was in 2008. For this special occasion I made her a "celebration of her life" movie. I canvassed all my family members for old photographs that I scanned of my siblings (on my free-with-a-Mac all-in-one

continued

scanner), her siblings and favorite family friends. I threw that into iMovie on my Mac (I would have used Final Cut Pro but that might have been overkill), added her favorite songs, burned some DVDs for the party, and my mother received the best birthday present *ever* (and hey, it may even increase my percentage of the inheritance).

Home Movie Do's & Don'ts

- *Do* use a real video camera, if you have one, instead of your digital camera.
- *Don't* approach *reluctant* people to participate (unless you *know* they're just playing hard-to-get—no one wants to watch someone who doesn't want to be taped).
- *Do* ask the hard questions even when you already know the answers.
- *Don't* chase your mom around the kitchen. Wait for her to sit down.
- *Do* get the fun b-roll of the kids playing in the backyard or sound bites of them talking to one another (this will help you significantly when you're editing—people love cute kids doing or saying cute things).
- *Do* get your aunt who thinks the entire family (including her own kids) are ne'er-do-wells (nothing is more entertaining than a drunk aunt talking sh*t about everyone else).
- *Do* immediately back up your work onto your laptop (your parents' twenty-fifth anniversary is only going to happen once).

THE FEATURE IN YOUR BACK POCKET

Once your short film is successful, many of you will turn your attention to getting your feature made. Your understanding of what works and what doesn't in a short film script is great preparation for a feature film career—because if you're ready to take on a feature, it's your feature script that's going to get you in the door. Know that writing a short script that you are in complete control of is very different from writing a script you want to pitch to studio executives. Mark and Jay—the Duplass brothers (*This Is John*, Sundance 2003; *Scrapple*, Sundance 2004, *The Intervention*, Clermont-Ferrand 2005; *The Puffy Chair*, Sundance 2007; *Baghead*, Sundance 2008) found this the most daunting aspect of their careers. Mark explains:

> "Uh, writing a good script is really really *really* hard. After having two shorts at Sundance, we figured it was time to try to make a feature. So, when Jay and I conceptualized *The Puffy Chair* we basically said, 'We know how to make a 10-minute film work, so let's just make about eight or nine 10-minute scenes in a row' and that's kind of what we did. We went for long scenes that we could improvise and make better as we shot. It's weird because we get a lot of compliments on the script for *The Puffy Chair* but the script itself wasn't that great. It was the performances, the direction, the improv, the editing—all of those things made the script look really good in the end.
>
> "Another thing we try to do is write very quickly. When we bang out a draft in a few days, writing in sequence from front to end, it's almost like your subconscious takes over and tells you how to pace the movie. Like all those days you spent in front of the TV watching HBO pays off at that point. Your intrinsic knowledge of movies and *what you wanna see next* kicks in and I think you get good pacing with this process. Then, you go back with the critical part of your brain and clean it all up and make it presentable.
>
> "Now, *presentable* is a tricky thing. If you want to sell your script, you kinda have to make it look and sound as

funny/dramatic/whatever as possible. The beats have to read more dramatically (or, ahem, less subtly) than you might prefer, but in our experience, getting a script greenlit in the studio system is kind of about making it a great read for the suits. It's an art form unto itself, and not one we're particularly fond of, but it is kind of a necessary evil until you've made five films and people really know what your tone is and what to expect from you.

"Then with *Baghead* we started the same way we always do. We banged out the first draft in a few days. It was really inspired and it had a ton of energy. But the ending wasn't what we wanted, and honestly, we waited around for a year for that ending to come to us. In the meantime, we passed the script around Hollywood to gauge people's interest in making it as a studio film, but nothing felt quite right. Eventually we found 'our' ending and ended up bending more than a couple of genres to get what we wanted, and we raised the money ourselves to make it immediately and without compromise."

Before it was announced that he won the Grand Jury Prize, Carter Smith (*Bugcrush*, Sundance 2006; *The Ruins*, 2008 DreamWorks production) and his feature script were accepted into the Sundance Screenwriters Lab. There is definitely something to be said about having a feature script that is similar in tone to the short you are shopping around.

Vanessa Coifman at Senator shares that one of the most important items a short filmmaker should have when going into a film executive meeting is a feature script. One feature Vanessa worked on, *Fireflies in the Garden*, was directed by Dennis Lee, who caught Vanessa's attention with his short film *Jesus Henry Christ*:

"It's one of those things where when someone does a good short and it actually manages to circulate, it's a better launching pad for a feature than a commercial or music video. We're in the market of discovering the next best director, and one of the best places to look is in the shorts. Because somebody put money into it that was probably their *own* money, so there's a care that goes into it that doesn't exist on a commercial or a music video; it's closer to them. And there's a pace and a tempo and a story that has to be told. If they do it well, it's the precursor of things to come."

But I know (and strongly believe) that for some of you making films, features are not the be-all and end-all of your career. Film-maker Kevin Everson (http://people.virginia.edu/~ke5d/) notes:

"For me, as an artist, it's your responsibility to keep making work as a citizen of the world. I'm not a doctor, but my way of healing folks is through entertainment and art and culture, so I feel it's my responsibility to my family, race, planet to keep doing stuff. People always ask me, are you going to turn your short into a feature? No. It's a piece of fuckin' art."

And now, let's talk short film structure.

2

Why 43-Minute Shorts Never Really Work (Script Structure)

Perhaps you're wondering what the difference between *story* and *structure* is. Simply put: Story is the WHAT and structure is the HOW (pacing/tempo). When you build a house you start with the what—four bedrooms, three baths, terrace, and kitchen. Then you move on to the how—your architectural design. We are at the design part of your script.

RESEARCH IS KEY

What can be one of the first steps you take to research and write a great script? Action. Throughout this book I am going to be repeating ad nauseam that you need to do your homework. Researching your story, your producer, your crew, your post, and your film's life once it's done is paramount to your success as a filmmaker.

Talmage Cooley is a great filmmaker who has had significant success with his odd storylines. *Pol Pot's Birthday* is a dark comedy that manages to be well written, beautifully shot, perfectly cast with a solid run time and payoff. His second, also very accomplished short, *Dimmer* (Sundance FF 2005), follows a blind street gang who terrorize their town on their bicycles. Talmage knows a thing or two about taking a story and laying it out successfully and the need for relentless research to accomplish this:

> "The biggest tricks to researching your script are watching a ton (not two or three but at least a hundred) of films that may have something in common with your film or may not. And photo books are one of the best resources of all, because they're the last 100 years of people documenting real life. The third thing, depending on where your film is set and what it's about, is to visit locations that are like the location you envision. If you have a scene set in a hair salon, go to a hair salon. Take pictures, and watch how things happen."

Action=Success. And the action that every filmmaker needs to take, whether you're making a narrative, documentary, animation, or experimental piece of work, is to research what has *already* been done, and researching what people actually do in hair salons (you think you know from memory, but you don't). Researching how twenty-seven-year-old women who work on Wall Street really dress in New York City. Researching the history of hand-drawn animation. Researching your grandmother's life story beyond what your mom has told you when she's had a little too much sherry.

By carefully researching your story you will save yourself time and money during production. This is critical. No matter what genre you're working within, when you thoroughly understand your characters and story, you'll be able to make the best film you can—even if it's not exactly how you originally envisioned it. It's a phenomenon that occurs in film all the time. You're making one film, yet another, different in many ways from your initial concept, emerges. If you're able to be flexible in everything from the plot points of your story to assembling the right cast and crew to last-minute changes in locations, to edits in post-production, it can often mean the difference between success and failure. Flexibility and adaptability relies *heavily* on knowing your story inside out.

Interesting & Fun Research Action

- Do an Internet search for Sundance shorts and *watch them*.
- Do an Internet search for filmmaker blogs and sign up for the ones that speak to you. Do the same for filmmaker newsletters. (Check out Resource Guide at the back of this book for ideas.)
- Start queuing up every short film compilation Netflix offers and *watch them*.
- Buy the last few years of Academy Award–nominated short film compilations. They've done it for 2009.

HOW SHORT IS SHORT?

Your script needs to be solid, economical, and fresh. Form follows function and short films, like short stories, have their very own style and pacing. No one could have written *Anna Karenina* in fourteen pages and most are not expecting *In the Mood for Love* in eight minutes.

The first item on the agenda is KISS—Keep It Simple Sister. So often I watch shorts that have complicated plotlines, multiple characters, and shifting locations, all crammed into twelve minutes. The short is so confusing you can almost see it on the actors' faces as they say their dialogue. The short film is successful economical storytelling. There are major aesthetic differences between Brent Green (*Hadacol Christmas*), Madeleine Olnek (*Hold Up, Waiting for Phyllis*), Joshua Leonard (*The Youth In Us, Beautiful Losers, The Blair Witch Project, Spectacular Regret*), and Carter Smith (*Bugcrush, The Ruins*) as filmmakers, as people, and in terms of what their ultimate filmmaker goals are. Yet they all have something in common—they have made films that have not only played at most of the major festivals but also received great critical acclaim.

Brent makes incredible 8-minute animation in his garage with a crazy Santa Claus as his protagonist. Madeleine shot her 8-minute DV film on the streets of Manhattan with three talented improv actors. Joshua wrote a beautifully tragic 12-minute story and wrangled two gifted actor colleagues to star in it. Carter, already a renowned fashion photographer and music video director, made an exceptional, creepy, gay horror film that was exquisitely shot, with teenagers who were at the beginning of their acting careers.

Bugcrush was 37 minutes long, an almost unheard-of length for a narrative short film. Smith shares:

> "*Bugcrush* was never a feature in my mind. Yes it was 37 minutes but that was all it was ever meant to be. It was based on a short story and I only wanted to make a short to get my feet wet. I wanted to show people that I had the skills to make a feature by creating a compelling *longer* short film that had three complete acts within the short film structure. I would hate to go back and tell that story again in a feature form—I think it would suck."

The bottom line with all of these films is that they are all economical in their storytelling. There isn't a scene that is clearly the director's favorite shot that he or she couldn't let go of in the edit suite. Every scene moves the story forward. Every single one, whether they were 8 minutes or 37. Director of photography Geary McLeod shares:

> "When filmmakers miss their mark it's hard to pinpoint why it doesn't work but I do know what that feels like—especially in a short film. You need to be concise. You need to figure out *exactly* what story you are telling. It's such a specific genre. Excess doesn't work. Every single frame has to work, it has to move the story forward. '*Economical*' is what short filmmakers need to remind themselves. Usually with a short film, it's your first time making a film, and you think, now this is the time to be self-indulgent. But it really isn't."

When I reached out to successful filmmakers about short film structure they all said you have to *understand* the form of shorts. Talmage Cooley (*Pol Pot's Birthday, Dimmer*) adds:

> "The easiest way to make this point is to make the analogy that a poem is structurally very different from a novel. You have to study the form and the syntax of short films to make sure that you are working in the right vernacular for that form. For example, with a poem there are certain expectations the audience has, there are certain limitations based on its length, and with a novel it's a whole different thing. And what I see all the time with short films is people trying to make a three-act story structure, and there's just not enough time to develop an emotional relationship to the characters in 10 minutes."

You may see a three-act structure in a longer short such as Smith's *Bugcrush*. However, the storyline, you have to admit— high school teens going on psychedelic trips using exotic bugs who lure another into their party with dark ulterior motives—is a fresh twist. Smith based his script on a beautifully crafted short story (written by Canadian artist Scott Treleaven) that lent itself to a three-act structure.

My advice for filmmakers trying to get their film onto the festival circuit? The more economical (read shorter) your film is, the easier it is to program. Short shorts can go in front of features or can round out a program and the mistakes you might make (shaky camera, not the greatest performance out of one of the actors, or shoddy set design) are *a lot* easier to forgive if you've managed to be economical *and* tell a great story.

Think about it. Most festivals have only a handful of programs dedicated to short films and most programmers want to help as many filmmakers as possible. If your pretty good short is eighteen minutes but includes about three minutes of fat and we're looking at two also pretty good shorts that total twelve minutes run time *sans* fat, guess who we're going to choose? Correct. The two films that respect the word "short" in short film.

As I noted earlier, between 2002 and 2007, less than five *narrative* shorts that were over thirty minutes screened at Sundance—*out of over five hundred* submitted I remember one was a gorgeous, dreamy non-linear film called *The Migration of Clouds* by Patrick Scott, and of course Carter Smith's *Bugcrush*.

We could often find a slot for an 8–12 minute film, but your 28-minute opus is going to sit on the "board" and probably not make the cut. It's a numbers game. As you've been told for years, bigger is not always better.

And I ask you—if your script is forty pages long (sometimes even twenty-page scripts fall under this spell), are you really developing a feature script, and will your short film based on this script actually look like a scene from *that* movie as opposed to a stand-alone piece of work? Don't do it. It's the hardest way to create a short—it rarely has a satisfying ending. Why? *Because there are fifty bloody minutes missing*—unbeknownst to the audience, who only sit there wondering where the ending to your film is. In the programming world, we often call these films "scene selects." They're not a whole film but a *selected scene* from a longer movie that you haven't shot yet. And since festivals are in the business of showing films and not scene selects . . . well, you get the picture.

Now what this doesn't preclude you from is taking a section of your feature script and re-creating a short story from it (as you lie in bed at night dreaming of someone giving you money to turn it into a feature. It could happen). Filmmakers successfully do it all the time. *Gowanus, Brooklyn*, written and directed by Ryan Fleck, went on to become *Half Nelson* (starring Ryan Gosling, Jeff Lima, and the brilliant Shareeka Epps). *Gowanus* was a self-contained story, with a great cast (Shareeka was also in the short) and a satisfying ending. Do some research. Find out what feature films began as short films and *study the form* and storyline of the short versus the feature.

CHARACTERS

As someone who's watched more than 15,000 films, I can tell within the first two minutes whether you really cared about the characters. Whether you made this film for yourself, because it came from your heart, because these characters had to be born, or because you thought it would get you into Clermont-Ferrand or Sundance. You and your pals may think you're being clever, but the truth always eventually comes to light.

I spoke to many filmmakers, festival programmers, and executives about this very topic. I want to be generous in this arena. I realize that we are bombarded daily with ultra-slick imagery, implausible plotlines, and celebrity cameos. You're out there watching short films either online or in festivals and you think, "I could do that." Yes, yes, you could. But not only has somebody *already* done that, but making it again, because you think this is the sort of stuff film festivals like, will not give you the tools you need to be a successful filmmaker. You need your own vision. This isn't just true in drama and documentaries. It's doubly true in comedy. Yes, we are all subjected to the formulaic comedy storylines and they're packed with familiar faces and big budgets, but you wouldn't be watching them if they didn't have one really special character that stands out. Someone created that character. And here is where I will agree that if they can do that, *you can do that.* A great book to check out is *The Tools of Screenwriting* by David Howard and Edward Mabley.

Creating characters is simple. What do they want? Who or where do they want it from? And how do they get it or do they get it at all? Why do they want it and, if they do get it, at what cost? Want, Where/Whom, Why.

You, as the screenwriter, need to know this more than anything else. I always tell my clients to write up a paragraph biography of each character. Have fun with it! Play around with them. This is the most control you're going to have making this short—writing the characters. What kind of underwear do they like to wear? What kind of ice cream is their favorite? Did they love their mom more than their dad?

The most believable characters in a film have a solid backstory that a capable actor allows to shine through with or without matching dialogue. This still holds true in animated films. When you're making a documentary *you already have the backstory,* and this can inform what kind of documentary you will create. And even if you're making a home movie, you must have an idea of how you want your story to be revealed.

DIALOGUE

I have actor friends who describe some of their work as being Exposition Fairies. This is the character who explains what the story is going to be about in order to help the filmmaker save time or money. Don't have $5k to show the audience how the guy jumped off the roof of a skyscraper? The actor won't do a full rape scene? Lead character is messed up from his parents' divorce? Have someone talk about it. If you've watched as many episodes of *Law & Order* as I have (yes, I've watched all of them, in back-to-back marathons, probably while I was supposed to be doing something else), you know exactly what an Exposition Fairy is. It's the cop (or best friend, or school principal, or computer geek) who walks in at the beginning of Scene 1 and tells the real detectives everything the writers don't have time to show you in 47 minutes. *She's been dead about a week, no I.D. but we found a wad of cash in her purse—all hundreds, and she's got a bar receipt from that fancy new restaurant down the street where mostly high-priced call girls and Wall Street guys hang out. Judging from the time on the receipt she left around 9 p.m. She's been raped and strangled to death with her pantyhose. We found a few fibers under her nails that we'll have sent over to forensics.*

Perfect. We now know what happened, who the detectives should interview first, and for sure those fibers will lead us to a guy who has done this before. We wait for the rest of the drama to transpire.

However, in screenwriting, if you write as if you have an unnatural affection for the Exposition Fairy characters, people may call you lazy or worse, boring. Be selective, *verrry* selective, on who in your film carries the exposition dialogue load and how necessary that load is in creating your story. If you have people *talking* about what your story is about as opposed to *showing* us what this story is about, then, my friend, what you have is a short story for a book, not a short film for the screen. Get busy and get creative.

Creativity and Your Budget

The old adage—write the film you want to write, shoot the film you are able, and edit the film you have—is true in both features

continued

and shorts. When I watched Joshua Leonard's *The Youth in Us*, the story was almost irrelevant. Why? Because I was visually captivated by the camera work, the production design, and most importantly the performances. I watched *The Youth in Us* in my living room on DVD, and then again I sat in the Eccles Theatre in Park City and watched it on the big screen; it had such a profound impact on me both times (and, yes, I cried *both* times).

Joshua shares his production values philosophy and the behind-the-scenes production realities of one of the truly pretty moments in *The Youth in Us*:

> "There's a flashback sequence that takes place in a snowy forest with deer, so originally we were going to shoot in a forest with snow machines, two young children, deer wranglers, until of course we realized that getting live deer was well over half the budget of our entire short film. Five grand a deer [laughs]. So my DP Horacio Marquínez and I started reconceiving, and that was based on shooting in a sound stage that we could get for free. Also working with my production designer, David Courtemarche, figuring out what was viable and how to take advantage of our budget restraints and not make it look like a compromise.
>
> "What I find with short films is that one of the greatest detriments to production is to try and make it look like something you don't actually have the resources to make. It always shows through and it's always fucking distracting. Not that you can't do a WWII short, but you have to figure out under which paradigm you're working, resource wise, and try to make it really doable, not trying to replicate something that's in your head. When we get into the production quality on something—if you're making a WWII short and you can do it in one dirty room and you tell a

continued

great story, no one's going to fault you that you weren't on a battlefield with 600 extras. But if you try to do it on a 'battlefield' and it looks like a playground and your seventeen extras are in mismatched costumes, it calls too much attention to itself. Reconceive the world, because at the end of the day, the story is most important."

Joshua's story worked creatively, without the flashbacks. However, this was one of the most crucial scenes in the film for him. The scene was successful because at no point were you, the audience, supposed to believe this was a *real forest,* with *real deer* or *real snow.* Josh blended in some magical realism using taxidermy, fake snow, and brilliant set design and lighting. By doing some creative research he was able to make that scene work . . . without the live deer at $5,000 a head.

Meredith Kadlec, Senior Vice President of Original Programming at here! Networks, had this to say on the subject:

"Don't fall into the trap of trying to prove how MUCH you can do, rather than how WELL you can do it. Don't write a script filled with tons of characters, crazy locations, etc., thinking you need to make your short film feel 'big.' It will be impossible to shoot and you'll be spreading yourself too thin for no reason. Spend more of your energy on *rewriting.* Shooting a truly brilliant script will do a lot more for your career than will the fancy production bells and whistles you load onto your credit cards."

WHAT'S THIS MOVIE ABOUT?

Am I four minutes into your 10-minute short and still don't know what the film is about? Back to the drawing board, my friend.

There is nothing more irritating than watching people do stuff for reasons unbeknownst to the audience until the film is almost over. You not only lose your audience but all the hard work of your actors is left floating in the galaxy. Why? Because we were so busy trying to figure out *why* they were doing or saying what they were doing or saying that by the time this is revealed to us we've *forgotten* what they did and what they said. (This is often the sad case for those films laden with Exposition Fairies.)

This is a common error many short filmmakers make in creating the setup for the rest of the film. A note my colleagues and I often wrote when taking notes on a short film submission was: *Took too long to get there. And when it got there the payoff wasn't worth it. You* might think something is cool or interesting enough to keep your audience wanting to know what happens next—but maybe it isn't. Cool photography or stellar editing does not a good movie make.

When structuring your script you need to grab the audience's attention in that first minute or two. If your film is a slightly longer doc (more than 15 minutes), you've got around 3 minutes to get us interested enough to watch the rest of your film. But you also want to be careful how you grab our attention.

This is where I believe making a short film is far more difficult than making a feature. You simply do not have the time to create a multi-layered, multi-character-driven work. Flashbacks (or flash forwards) eat up time, slow opening scenes eat up time, complicated relationship setups eat up time—and this is a short film.

Where some filmmakers have succeeded is by setting up the story under opening credits. Sometimes it works (like with Leonard's *The Youth in Us*) but *most times* it doesn't. I hate opening credits in a short film unless you are truly setting up the story. If you lay opening credits over slick photography because you thought it would be cool or you didn't know what else to do with all that b-roll your DP shot, cut it out now. When I asked

Kim Yutani, Sundance Shorts Programmer and Director of Programming at Outfest, what she wished every filmmaker would do, she told me one of her wishes:

> "All I want to do is watch your movie. It shouldn't have color bars, a minute of black or opening credits—nobody even knows who these people or production companies are! And I shouldn't have to scroll through a menu. I should be able to put your DVD into my machine and your movie should start playing. Period."

I know, I know. You spent four hours figuring out how to create a cool menu in DVD Studio Pro. But remember, from moment one you want your film to tell your story. Do you really want your story to begin with cliché filmmaker self-indulgence?

Filmmaker Danielle Lurie (*In the Morning*, Sundance 2005) shares:

> "The best thing you can do for your audience is to give them something delicious right from the start. Something shocking, something unnerving, or if you're really good—something they've never seen before. Then they're hooked, and are in for the next five, ten, fifteen minutes. People watch shorts because they are short—if your short lags in the beginning, it's not going to feel short and people who signed up to watch something short will feel cheated; on the flip side, if your film hits the ground running from second one, your short will seem even shorter than it is and you'll be home free. Most filmmakers are under the impression that for a short film to work, it needs to have an excellent twist at the end—and I agree with that for the most part—but what's even more crucial is that there be something exciting to hook them in the beginning—no matter how great a twist is, if the audience has left the theater it won't matter. In my

short film, *In the Morning,* the first climactic moment was initially written to happen a few minutes in, but I decided to start with it instead in order to get my audience hooked right away. I rearranged the story so that I placed this exciting scene in the first ten seconds and then used flashbacks to it later in the script which I think kept the audience more engaged than they would have been otherwise. My short was ten minutes, but people always said it felt half that length."

But do not rely on flashbacks to tell your story if your story doesn't work without them. With my programmer hat on, I would say that both *In the Morning* and *The Youth in Us* would have worked with or without the flashbacks because the story was *already* there making the flashbacks a creative choice and not something pertinent to the audience understanding the film.

I cannot stress enough how important short film structure is to your success. As a short filmmaker, you are bound by a time limit. You can take 10 minutes to cultivate a character in a feature. In a short that's most (if not *all*) of your allotted time. Break down your script in a similar fashion to breaking down a feature script. If your film is 12 minutes long, at what point in the script do you show us the story's main arc? Believe me, it's not on page 7.

When I first wrote the script for *Dani and Alice* there were four pages of setup. Who these characters were, how they got dressed for the evening, what perfume they chose, blah blah blah. After sending it out to a few friends for notes they all came back saying, "Start the story faster. Cut out the fat." Keeping in mind that this is a *visual* medium, I gave the audience *visual cues* as to who these people were in minute 1. I moved the drama to that first 2 minutes. You already *knew* who these people were based on how they were dressed, who was driving, their body language, and of course, through the dialogue. Plus, adding all that setup I originally planned for would have added a minimum of another half-day of shooting that my budget could not support. That film wouldn't have played at ten festivals never mind over 100, had it begun with those first 4 self-indulgent minutes.

WHAT MAKES STRUCTURE RULES DIFFERENT FOR DOCUMENTARIES?

With docs, filmmakers often make a similar mistake, believing that they have more time to allow the story to unfold than they actually do to keep the audience's interest. Diane Weyermann notes:

> "Something that can get lost in documentaries is that, certainly for beginning filmmakers out in the field, they think they have a really compelling story or subject, and they go out and film it in this straightforward documentation way. But that's also a real issue that filmmakers should consider very deeply *before* embarking to make that film. You are a storyteller, a filmmaker, you are using a visual creative medium, how do you take that story and move it beyond pure documentation into filmmaking storytelling with full use of the visual aesthetic to engage people. Editing, music, the look of the film. I think that to the extent that docs have become more popular in the last eight to ten years is largely connected to what I believe is the storytelling and aesthetic qualities that have been brought to the field. There is no longer this feeling that docs are like medicine, they're good for you, or perhaps they're educational, but that they're not interesting, engaging, surprising, or emotionally moving in the filmic storytelling ways. How it's shot, how it's edited, constructed, how graphics are used; there are so many different *important* elements to focus on."

A truly great gift that documentary filmmakers shared with me is that more often than not, they began to make a documentary about one thing but once in production (or even later in the edit) they realized their film was about something else entirely. Tia Lessin (*Bowling for Columbine, Fahrenheit 9/11, Trouble the Water*) is an extraordinary documentary filmmaker and producer who experienced this while making *Trouble the Water*, which won both the Sundance and Full Frame Documentary Grand Jury Prize (www.elsewherefilms.org):

"The heart of any good story—whether fiction or nonfiction—is strong characters and during those first few days of shooting in the aftermath of [Hurricane] Katrina, my partner Carl [Deal] and I were looking for characters that could lead us through the story. We were focusing on soldiers from the Louisiana National Guard who were returning from Baghdad so we could make the connection between the Iraq war and the failed government response along the Gulf Coast. Our eyes and ears were open, trying to respond to what was going on in the moment, so when Kimberly and Scott Roberts approached us at the Red Cross Shelter across the parking lot from the National Guard Armory we redirected our cameras and our story.

"Part of what was appealing to us about Kimberly and Scott as characters was they belied the stereotypes we were seeing on TV at that time—racist depictions of New Orleans' African American residents as either rampaging, criminal looters or helpless victims. Though they called themselves street hustlers, Kimberly and Scott are also talented, resourceful, and deeply sympathetic people. They are no one's victims.

"After a couple of days, Kimberly showed us the raw home movie footage that she shot the day before and the day of the storm. Carl and I felt surprise and outrage, and were moved to tears and, thanks to her real-time voiceover, to laughter; we knew that her home movies could fill in the blanks before the storm, and our footage could tell the story in the aftermath. We didn't know how their story would turn out, and that was part of the appeal."

And when you're trying to get your documentary into festivals, Basil Tskiokos, Artistic Director of NewFest (www.newfest .org) and Sundance U.S. Documentary Features Programming Associate, shares:

"Documentary or narrative, the biggest challenge for any film is the story, and the danger when making a documentary is, since it's 'true,' finding the story, or better yet, finding the right way to tell the story can be very elusive. Filmmakers can get too close to their subjects and lose objectivity, or they can simply allow themselves and their films to meander. Beyond this, of course, is the tendency to rely too much on talking heads, a trap most beginning documentarians fall into."

Know Your Story Better Than You Know Yourself

Prolific filmmaker/performance artist and author Miranda July has created over ten marvelous short film works. She had captivated audiences with her non-linear performance film art for decades and was trying to get her feature made. She was rejected twice at the Sundance Screenwriters Lab before her script was selected and subsequently she debuted it at Sundance in 2005. *Me and You and Everyone We Know* won the 2005 Sundance Special Jury Prize, the coveted 2005 Camera D'Or at Cannes, and many other awards. She also wrote the

continued

short script *Are You the Favorite Person of Anyone?* that we featured in the 2005 Sundance Festival in the Short Film Competition. Miranda talks about her creative process:

"I had been writing and performing [both sides of] dialogues for a long time [in my performances] when I began to write a feature script for the first time. So dialogue came easily, and I performed it as I typed it, all the parts. And when I began working with my DP Chuy Chavez, I acted out the whole movie for him, like a one-woman show, so he could feel what was most important to me in each scene.

"Also, if you have connected with an audience live, in person, then you have a very visceral knowledge of their attention, and *what it feels like when it wanders*. That's very useful knowledge to have.

"Most importantly: Performance is the realm in which I feel most free—in part because the medium is inherently experimental—but also, at this point, because it is cheap or free, and does not revolve around critical success in the way a movie or book does. It is good to have an arena that is free of all that. The feature film I am working on now evolved out of a performance, which is the only way it could have happened I think. I had to return to a creative land that pre-dated *Me and You and Everyone We Know*.

"As well . . . so many of the things I did in *Me and You* weren't new to me: working with children, directing myself, the whole process of writing, shooting, editing, scoring. I had done all that many times and it was really only a matter of scale when I did the feature."

Genius. She knew exactly what she wanted before she got on set. She made a film about something she knew a lot about. Learn from that—it's one of the most important elements to being

continued

a great director. Know more about your story than anyone else involved.

When I was prepping *Dani and Alice,* I acted out the entire script with fellow filmmaker Trish Doolan (*April's Shower, Bug in My Ear, What's True*), who is also a trained actor. We played all the parts, moved furniture around in her living room creating the entire set. By doing this work, I went back and made the script even tighter once I realized what no longer needed to be there. Remember our key word, "economical." And more importantly, once on set, when camera moves had to be condensed due to time restrictions, *I knew what the essence of the scene was,* so it didn't matter if they were sitting, standing, or in a stationary car.

And don't think that only applies to professional filmmakers. If the *only* person willing to speak on camera is Aunt Judy, then you need to be prepared to steer her in the direction you want this home movie to go and have fun with your editing by highlighting exactly how cool she really is.

I'M GONNA GET DISCOVERED!

One sign of talent that agents look for is the ability to recognize what an appropriate subject for a short film is. It shows good judgment. If you get incredible performances and it looks great but the story is unsatisfying in a 15–20 minute format, does that inspire faith in your ability to make the thousands of decisions required for a two-hour feature? No, it doesn't.

Oh, but you cry, "It's a calling card film! I'm trying to get a manager or agent to see that I can direct this kind of high concept film."

Yes, there are agents out there looking for up-and-coming

directors who can manage these kinds of films. *However,* you still have to have believable characters doing believable things in a believable world. These people are not idiots. There are thousands of you out there sending in demo reels. They are looking for that filmmaker who can not only make a great genre film but is also a great storyteller. A great storyteller with an *original* vision.

Like I said, if you make a film that looks like you followed Wong Kar-wai around for a year, the agent is going to move on to someone who has taken a risk creatively and has their own vision to share with an audience. I mean, it seems obvious to me—Wong Kar-wai is already making films, great films. You coming along and making a similar, if not the same film, seems . . . well it seems kinda redundant (read dumb). The truer you stay to your vision, the more likely someone in a position to help you further your career, like an agent, will be to take notice. Craig Kestel is not only an agent at the William Morris Agency, which is one of the largest talent agencies in the world, he is also a huge champion of the short filmmaker. Craig adds his perspective:

"I can't speak for all agents but when I'm watching shorts I'm not only looking for those that are glossy, studio-friendly productions or what we perceive as studio-friendly productions. Actually it's usually not. I have to connect to the character, or the look, or the style. One of my clients, Dito Montiel, made an experimental short which was shots of the New York City skyline with recited poetry and if you see his first feature *A Guide to Recognizing Your Saints* [starring Dianne Wiest and Robert Downey, Jr.] that won two awards at Sundance, you can see the threads of his short film style in his feature. There's an example of experimental shorts translating well into a great independent feature, and now he's making his first studio feature. Another short I flipped for was *Gowanus, Brooklyn,* that also won Sundance, that Ryan [Fleck] and Anna [Boden] were able to translate into an award-winning independent feature *Half Nelson.* A lot of feature filmmakers' style points to their first short film. For me it's just more about style; it's the reaction to the first film, and the storytelling. I'm into glossy, cool things too, but at the core of what I'm attracted to—it's the story."

So now you have your story and the structure to your film. It's time to find a producer and crew up.

3

How to Avoid Kicking Your Producer in the Throat

The producer on a film, any film, is the most important person involved. Yes, you're the director and it's your vision, but *nothing* happens (and if it does it usually doesn't happen *as well*) without a solid producer overseeing your project. I've met some incredible creative producers who helped the filmmaker craft a successful film by not only becoming a creative partner but also by being physical producers as well, someone who takes care of the *hundreds* of details required to create an accomplished work. In shorts, since you may only have one person producing your film, you'd do yourself a huge favor by choosing someone who can do both.

Filmmaker Abigail Severance (*Siren*, Sundance 2002; *Come Nightfall*, Sundance 2003; *Saint Henry*, Spotlight Award—Directing 2005; *The Summer We Drowned*, Screenwriting Lab selection FIND 2007) shares her experiences:

"Producing a short film is a strange job because it carries very little of the glamour of filmmaking that people associate with movies, Hollywood, etc. When I asked a friend who had produced one short for me to do the same on my new film, she said kindly but firmly, 'Oh you mean be your key set PA? I love you, but no thanks.' Finding a good producer who is willing and able to organize volunteers, get stuff donated, and still have the Big Picture in mind is difficult. Then on my third short *Saint Henry,* I found a great, energetic creative producer who was *very* green when it came to the actual production side. About three weeks before the shoot, I was in a panic because so many things had yet to come together. Since most directors are in a constant state of panic at that stage, I couldn't get her to take my particular panic seriously so I asked an experienced producer friend to meet with us and she spent three hours running through a list of forty-seven items that needed attention. By the end of the meeting, my sweet, energetic producer was white as a sheet. The magnitude of work had finally dawned on her. To her credit, she panicked only briefly, then kicked into high gear and pulled everything off. Not as cheaply as I would have liked, but she got the work done. Often we are dealing with people who are trying out the idea of being a producer but don't really know the nuts & bolts and short film producing is ALL nuts & bolts."

Over the years at Sundance and other film-related jobs, I've had the pleasure of meeting many film producers who believed in the director, loved the script, were able to help the project get financing and casting, and facilitated post-production. Some were already feature producers who sensed that the filmmaker had a great feature script they'd eventually like to produce once the director had earned some chops making a short. This is a great scenario because the producer and director get to practice working together on a small scale before throwing themselves into the grueling two-year feature film process.

Now, I've also met producers who did nothing but hinder a project. They lied about their connections, they undermined the director's vision, they made it seem as though the project couldn't have happened without them, and finally, they were awful to deal with at the festival (or with the crew, the vendors, the talent, and the post houses). They spend a lot of time talking and very little doing. Do not be fooled.

HOW TO SPOT A BAD PRODUCER FROM A MILE AWAY

I personally have never had a "bad" producer. I thought the best way to find out what a bad producer looks like is to ask a *good* one. Steak House, of Steakhaus Productions (www.steakhaus .com), who has produced over ten shorts including *Phase 5* (Sundance 2003) and *Billy's Dad Is a Fudge-Packer* (Sundance 2005), alongside five features including the indie feature hit *By Hook or By Crook* (Sundance 2002) and *For the Love of Dolly* (Wolfe, released summer 2008) tipped me off to some telltale signs of a bad producer:

> "Well, here's what I would say—you want someone who is honest. The telltale sign of a bad producer that is easiest to see at the beginning is lying. You catch people in these weird little lies, exaggerations and stuff like that. Okay, granted, everyone tells exaggerated stories a little bit, you ramp up a story, that's just talking. But when you catch people in straight-up lying the one thing I've learned is to stop it early. A week goes by and nothing of what they claimed they could accomplish got done. Another week goes by and still nothing's done? They are never going to do anything for you. But, let's be clear. If they tell you they can't do anything for you until March and you're calling every day in February . . . be realistic on your side and on their side."

Filmmaker Madeleine Olnek (*Hold Up, Make Room for Phyllis, Countertransference*) produced her own short *Hold Up* and has also worked with additional producers on other projects. Madeleine shares her thoughts about the differences between a good producer and a not-so-good producer:

> "The most important thing a producer should have is an eye for detail. An eye for detail, a memory of detail, because the ability to be proactive is enabled by knowledge, comprised of details. A good producer also understands the enormous pressures a director is under and does everything they can to take extra stresses off the director, so they can direct the movie well. I think good producers are 'hands on' people; there is a lot of legwork involved in producing a short. Getting someone to produce who sees their task as delegating, and the to-do list as 'errands' (when getting those things done absolutely affects the quality of what ends up on the screen) is just someone who is going to put more on your plate. When people are, essentially, being paid in credits, it is very hard to find people for the producer to delegate their job to who are competent; competent people quickly size up the fact that they are doing the work just for someone else to get the credit and they eventually quit. And usually these delegatory types of producers exacerbate the situation with intentionally high-profile entrances and parade around the set for five minutes (as if that does anything) on their way to martinis (which they let everyone know about). And if a producer is not really going to be involved in a hands-on way in the everyday nitty-gritty of getting a movie together, what's the point of them working on the movie? You'd be better off doing it yourself and getting credit for the 'errands' you will inevitably be running anyway."

HIGH-PROFILE NAME PRODUCERS

I have watched many filmmakers holding out for the big-name producer only for that producer to, months down the road, have to pull out because something bigger has come along. If you're going the "name" producer route make sure you have solid backup.

It is possible to get a seasoned producer to take a look at your project. This is another arena where networking comes in. Ask around in the network of industry contacts that you will develop (or are in the process of developing, as this community will expand and contract constantly) and start interviewing people. No, you're probably not going to get Effie T. Brown or Allen Bain straight out of the gate. But try to.

Aim high. Higher, dude.

And, yes, I said start *interviewing*.

When I was in the market for a producer I found that even people much higher up the food chain than I were very excited to meet first and discuss the project to ensure we were a good fit. In fact, it would seem unprofessional and naive for you not to want to set up a "get to know you" interview before forging ahead in such an important partnership.

Generally speaking, the more seasoned the producer you attach to your film, the more producing you are going to have to do yourself. So you should make sure to have another producer on board who can address the details of your shoot. No, seasoned producers are not slackers. However, they are usually very busy and not available to find out if you can get a free camera package or investigate the best location for you to use, or to help with the breakdown of your budget.

I got very lucky and had the undeniably gifted Effie T. Brown as my producer on *Dani and Alice*. I was having drinks with Effie and Susan O'Leary, who was then the Director of Fox

Searchlight's director's lab, *foxsearchlab*. There was always free Absolut vodka flowing in the Red Room during the Los Angeles Film Festival the year I was programming there (during my Sundance off-season). Late into the evening I was sitting with Effie and Susan, and Susan was relentless about me taking action on my own filmmaking aspirations and so I just blurted it out, "Yes, yes, I'll make it this year . . . will you guys produce it?" They both gave me a resounding YES. Susan invited my script into the *foxsearchlab* and Effie came on board as the producer. (Thank you Absolut!) Effie shares her wisdom:

> "I would give you the same advice on a short film as a feature film. It's the same relationship. People don't realize that making a short film and making a feature are the same amount of work. And oftentimes making a feature is actually easier, because you have more of a budget for it. When you're looking for a producer, know that you're going to be in bed with that person for at least a year. So you need someone with a like mind, a like vision, *and* a like temperament. No matter how fabulous you think you are, there will always be a crisis. And you need to turn to someone who can handle the crisis with you. It's a combination of creative vision, temperament, and crisis management. Those three things are really important in a director. *And* probably more so in producers. When I was coming up, I was a line producer, and as a line producer I was beholden to the plan that I was mapping out and *not* beholden to the creative vision. So my relationship with directors was often, at the beginning of my career, antagonistic. Then as I climbed up the ladder, I realized that while money dictates creative, creative also helps you with your bottom line."

By using Effie's name and contacts alone, I was a million miles ahead of the game. By having Susan's support at *foxsearchlab*, I was able to shoot on 35mm. As I noted, when you get a big-name producer you may also need to find another producer(s) to do the heavy lifting (budgets, locations, etc.). I found top-notch Christo DiMassis and Roger Mayer of Brooklyn Reptyle Productions and an outstanding production manager, Tracy Lynn Smith, through Jacques Thelemaque at Filmmakers Alliance (www.filmmakers alliance.org). Effie and I agreed that we couldn't have made that film without those three pulling in favors, working twenty-hour days, and keeping the rest of the crew laughing and motivated. And of course, having director of photography Geary McLeod pulling in favors of his own, and his very capable camera crew making magic on-set was invaluable.

HOW WILL I KNOW IF THIS IS THE RIGHT PRODUCER?

The first thing I'll tell you is there aren't many (any?) producers I know out there who help directors finance their shorts, and by this I mean they are not going to find you cash money. However, they should be able to get you donated stuff and a free or close-to-free crew, but the actual cash you need to go into production will be all on you.

Good places to start looking for a producer is by inquiring with other filmmakers and checking out your local filmmaker group (e.g., IFP in New York provides immeasurable support and references for budding filmmakers, as does Filmmakers Alliance in Los Angeles). Most cities, big and small, all over the world have some sort of filmmaker networking organization.

Film festivals are another great place where you can meet producers who have already accomplished what you are trying to: get a film made that gets selected for a festival. Just make sure to talk to the director they are there with. Maybe that film got made with very little help from the person who was given a producer credit and you'd want to know that before asking them to come onto your project only to find yourself alone doing all of the work.

MAYBE MY BEST FRIEND JACK
CAN BE MY PRODUCER!

The relationship between a producer and director can get contentious. Okay, it's pretty much always a little contentious, no matter how much love you share. You want a crane shot, which they know you don't have and will not be able to find the money in the budget for (plus crane shots in shorts are crazy, uh, I mean *unnecessary*). You think shooting digitally instead of 35 mm will cramp your creative style and they know that it's your only choice budget-wise (more on this in Chapter 4). You want to keep the beach scene at dusk and it's their job to break it to you that scheduling-wise that's impossible. Maybe you're thinking to yourself, "I'll look within my group of friends and find someone who really believes in me and my movie."

Hmm, I made this very decision with *Dani and Alice* when I begged my friend Steak House to come on board. I thought she'd be great, having been a line producer for many years. I loved her energy, talent, and sense of humor no matter how challenging things got. However, bad timing on both our parts made this a match made in filmmaking hell. Fortunately, our love and respect for each other made the make-up easy and we'll be friends forever. Steak talks about some of her wisdom gained from ten years and ten-plus short films alongside several independent features wisdom with us:

> "I like to call it 'crushing my sparkle.' I avoid working with people who crush my sparkle and directors should also be looking for producers who don't do that to them. Essentially, you're looking for someone who has *time* to devote to your project. Someone with a DIY [do-it-yourself] sensibility. Someone who is not afraid to ask for things, to make those cold calls to get stuff for free, because you're probably not going to get some super-experienced producer to help

you accomplish this kind of work at this stage in your career."

Finding an impartial objective person to share this creative vision with you is a *must*. If you think one of your friends is the right person for the job, go out and ask another filmmaker who also thought that and see if they're still friends with that producer—if they can even stand to be in the same room together. Or if that producer is still among the living. Or if your director friend still gets a tic in her face every time someone puts on their slippers (see page 58).

It's imperative to be realistic with your expectations as to what a producer can and cannot do for you and your short film. Keep in mind that filmmaking is a business for most producers. As the director you have a lot more to gain (and lose) than anyone else on this project, as Steak reminds us:

> "No one cares about your project as much as you do—no matter what they say. That's another director delusional moment, 'Oh everyone is going to work as hard on my film as I am.' No. No they're not. Only the director is going to work that hard. Then the producer, then the director of photography, then the editor and so on. But as a director it is *you* who is going to follow this movie all the way through because with a short there's not a lot for the producer to do after the principal shooting. Maybe as your producer I can get you a discounted telecine or hook you up with a few editors I know, but most of the post-production will be done by you or if you have money to hire a post supervisor, by them."

I CAN BE MY OWN PRODUCER!

Uh, no, no you can't. And, besides, why would you want to if you've got people willing to help? Believe me, when I watch a film where the director lists themselves as the writer/director/producer/editor—it shows. There are things missing . . . like, ahem, good performances. How can you focus on actors when you're constantly being pulled out of your director role putting out production fires?

I could list the thousands of filmmakers who were emotionally scarred for life from producing their own film but instead I'll keep it real by reliving the production of my last short, *Happy Birthday*.

I had this great idea for a short that I wanted to get done before 2007 ended. I enlisted some help to get the first draft of the script done and then I contacted the actors I knew I wanted to cast. I thought, "I don't need to find a producer! I'll do it all myself! I'm writing a book about it for crying out loud, I can do this!"

Nonsense.

It's the job of the director to DIRECT actors. Seems simple, but we all seem to forget that that is our actual job. And on a good set, it's your only job. There is no more collaborative work than filmmaking (except launching astronauts to the moon), and if you think you can do it all yourself—think again.

Wait! What Does A Producer Do?

J.D. DiSalvatore, an award-winning producer, has made her share of short and feature films (*Gay Propaganda, Shelter*). She has a great Web site dedicated to indie film gossip (www.thesmokingcocktail.com), and when I asked her to answer the question, "What Does A Producer Do?" she responded with her tongue-in-cheek version of what she does for a living:

J.D. DiSalvatore's "What A Producer Does" List

♦ Find good scripts (this task resembles any Indiana Jones movie when he's looking for buried treasure while being chased by Nazis).

continued

◆ Convince someone with money to invest in the script (it helps if one took drama in high school, as this involves a lot of dog and pony show tactics and tap dancing).

◆ Listen to a director throw phrases around like, "My vision," usually with the request for some profoundly expensive and useless piece of equipment.

◆ Try not to develop a Xanax addiction while waiting for your funding from investors to drop into your bank account.

◆ Find your screenwriter at noon facedown in a glass of gin at Musso and Frank's mumbling, "They're ruining my script."

◆ Ask your lawyer to ask their lawyer what it felt like when his soul slipped out of his body, and what it was like to actually meet Satan.

◆ Tell the actresses they're pretty.

◆ Tell the actors they're pretty.

◆ Tell the studio executives they're pretty. And smart. They really like that.

◆ Smile and nod when studio executives give you notes, generally trying to change your pensive tone poem on social inequality into a musical version of *Porky's*.

◆ Smile and nod when one of your investors insists on having their boyfriend in the movie.

◆ Listen to the director yell and scream when you pass the above message on.

◆ Hire and negotiate everyone's contract (which is why my hair is gray).

◆ Listen to more of "my vision" with a request to shut down several streets of downtown LA—*for a full day*.

◆ Send expensive bottles of liquor to all your vendors.

◆ Try not to say ANYTHING when your film executive says, "No, I've never heard of *Citizen Kane*."

◆ Tell your DP there's no more money in the budget for the camera department.

continued

- Tell the art department there's no more money in the budget for them.
- Tell the visual effects department there's no more money in the budget for them.
- More of "my vision" when the director wants "one little scene" and "only needs it shut down for a few hours" when referring to LAX on a Friday afternoon of Labor Day weekend.
- Repeat to yourself "I will not cry, I will not cry," when the driver forgets to engage the emergency brake and the entire prop truck slides off the cliffs of Malibu Canyon into the Pacific Ocean.
- Try not to develop a Xanax addiction when your lead actor finds out about the SAG clause that states he doesn't really need to do nudity.
- Tell the Teamsters you're only shooting a $40,000 mini dv film with money your mom gave you.
- Send expensive bottles of liquor to the buyers at all the distribution companies.
- Hold your editor's hand during the first three weeks of post while the director does his/her cut, while reiterating, "I know, you'll get it soon, and *you'll* be able to do it right."
- Persuade director not to cut out all the scenes with the actor that wouldn't sleep with him/her on set.
- Try not to develop a Xanax addiction when you find out your investor's boyfriend, who you cast in the movie, has run off to Mexico with one of the *other* actors from set.
- Tell editor to remove all scenes from film with investor's boyfriend. And the actor he ran off with.
- Send every PA and intern you have to the Chateau Marmont bungalows and pull your composer out of his ten-day coke binge, send the girls home, and tell him the soundtrack is due.

continued

- Get the audience drunk on champagne at your first screening, prior of course.
- Tell film festival programmers they're pretty.
- Try not to develop a Xanax addiction when your film print comes back with the entire sound off by three seconds.
- Trade gossip about Drew Barrymore to *US Weekly* in exchange for a mention of your film's theatrical opening.
- Convince your lead actor to get caught in a DUI or prostitution scandal just prior to your film's release. Photographed with Paris Hilton, also a plus.
- Strongly suggest to your prettiest actor that he "drop the soap" when he hand-delivers the preview DVD of the movie to Perez Hilton.
- Send anonymous e-mails to reviewers who panned your film asking them what the highest grade of public school was they completed.
- Try not to develop a Xanax addiction while waiting for the first Box Office results.
- Try to close your next movie deal before said Box Office results hit the trades.
- Repeat above steps.

Now, what happened in pre-production, production, and post with me as the main producer could have easily been avoided had I had someone in that essential role. When you're thinking in a vacuum, making all the decisions yourself, you tend to lose sight of the details. And as we've learned, filmmaking is *all* in the details. Instead of burning myself out on the phone, in meetings, and schlepping equipment all over Manhattan and Brooklyn, I could have been doing the only job I was actually there to do on this film: Direct the actors and quality control the end product. Sure, I know a lot about filmmaking and could certainly produce *someone else*'s work, but in the future I will never work on my own film without another producer on board from the beginning. Ever.

If you watch *Happy Birthday* you'll see that I was able to make a fun short with great performances that played all over the world, garnered both DVD release and broadcast distribution both here at home and internationally. But this was only because producer Jon Johnson came on board, scouting locations and finding private money, and my fantastic first AD/production manager, Marina Guzman, took over as producer once it became clear that I was wearing one hat too many.

Listen to people who know more than you, have done way more than you have, and are really, really, really successful at it. Making a short film isn't a personality contest, but if you don't heed your grandmother's advice, "You get more bees with honey," you may find yourself very, very sad and very, very, *very* alone by the time you get to post-production.

I say this from experience—don't be a know-it-all. A director is set up to be the captain of the ship from the outset, and for some of us that means having to know everything! But what if you don't? (I mean, how could you?! This is your first movie!) So there I was, thinking (and acting like) I knew everything about my film there was to know—but luckily I had that arrogant attitude quickly adjusted by Effie during pre-production (let's just say there was a slipper involved—flying across the room barely missing my head). She was, of course, right, and I needed to step back and listen to someone who had done this many times before with fantastic results. Effie talks about the director/producer relationship:

> "It took a while, but I finally learned that it always gets to
> the point where when you don't have the answers, instead of
> freaking out, you just say, 'I don't know. Let me go find out
> about that.' That's the thing that saves my ass every time.

Admitting I don't know everything and going and finding out those answers. And, of course, being a good producer is being able to tell people something in a way that they can hear it. I learned you can come at somebody from a different entry point without being aggressive and still get your point across without making them feel defensive or challenging their creative vision. It's communication and human psychology. You have to be able to read people. . . . I can't stress enough, it *really* is like dating. When you find someone you work well with, you just stick with it. It's like a marriage that works."

Heed the advice in this chapter and I can almost promise you and your project will find the right producer.

4

Money, Money, Money

PART 1—BUDGETS

Now, some of you are making shorts to make people laugh (mostly your friends or family), some of you are making one to get your feature made, some of you are making one as a pilot to sell to a television network, and some of you are making one just to practice your directing chops with the hope of doing well and getting your name out there on the festival circuit and perhaps even getting distribution. All of these different motivations are great ones, and will require different budget ranges.

Your budget decisions will be dependent not on only what your story is, but also what format you plan to shoot on. This is why you want to *research* your film in its script stage so you know *exactly* how much money you need to raise to accomplish your goal. Remember the $3,000 it was going to cost me to have my actors talking and driving?

I always knew I wanted to shoot on 35mm. What I did have to back up that goal was two donated 35mm camera packages from Panavision, a bunch of low-cost film from Chris Russo at Kodak, a great deal at Color by Deluxe (working with Charles McCusker Sr. and Marc Fishman), free locations, and the entire crew that worked for free, so my budget decisions were based on a very small amount of money that I'd been given from *foxsearchlab* and what I'd raised privately.

However, when I got to the pre-production table with what I thought was oodles of cash and an overwhelming amount of donated product, both Effie and Steak set me straight about how much things *really* cost even when you get a load of it for free. They didn't deter my ultimate goals, but what they did do, as producers, was provide me with a fundraising goal to meet if I was going to get all of the creative aspects of my film accomplished. Their input was invaluable. That's why your producer is the *first* person to hire!

There are several ranges of budgets for shorts. Later in this chapter you will get a look at some sample budgets.

- $0–$1,000 range
- $1,000–$5,000 range
- $5,000–$20,000 range
- $20,000–$40,000 range
- $40,000–$75,000 range
- above $75,000

The super-low-budget range ($0–$1,000) is shot on cheap video, self-edited, unpaid crew, you and your pals are the talent, self-sourced locations (your friend's backyard). This is the film that many people think they should start with. I disagree. This is exactly the type of film I warn people against making because of poor production values and unqualified performances (unless of course you're just making a short to throw up on a user-generated content site, like YouTube, to entertain your friends). Sure, there are exceptions within this budget range; just keep in mind that they are few and far between and yours probably isn't one of them.

A great exception I'd like to note is the Duplass Brothers' *This Is John*. This was an eight-minute film made on video starring one brother, Mark, shot by the other brother, Jay, in their kitchen, and self-edited. The film is a tribute to the meltdown some of us (Oh, come on! *Most* of us) have when recording our outgoing voice-mail message. A universal story, a pitch-perfect performance by Mark, appropriate editing and sound design made this a great one-act film. They made it after ten years of thugging it out writing feature scripts with little success, living in Austin, TX, in deep *filmmaker depression* (if you don't know what this is yet, you soon will). They decided to get off the couch and shoot something. Anything. And it paid off. It cost them $3 for the tape stock (they owned the video camera and the bottle of wine you see in the film was an old empty one).

What works about this short, and others like it, is the fact that the medium (video without light package) matched the story (guy in a kitchen recording outgoing voice mail) matched the length (under eight minutes *with* credits), which also matched the budget (under $1,000).

If Mark and Jay attempted to make this film with four locations, five actors, and a lengthy dialogue-filled scene with the same budget and production values, *This Is John* would have joined the ranks of the 4,400 other filmmakers who received rejection letters at Sundance that year.

The next couple of budget ranges tend to be where most short films should fall. I reached out to a prolific producer, Steak House (www.steakhaus.com), and she breaks down the budgeting process of short films:

> "What most wannabe filmmakers don't want to know is that to make a high production value, well scheduled, confident *narrative* short film you need a budget of about $20,000. That said, you can often rely on your producer or other crew members—sometimes even actors know someone who

knows someone—to help you get equipment and crew for free. But even with free crew, a 2–3 location narrative short with a solid camera package, professional actors, and crew runs at the very least $10k and then there's post-production. And you should *always* be budgeting your film to include post. Once you move down from that number you have to start rethinking your script, number of locations, camera and light packages and *where you think this film will screen*. I've had many filmmakers hand me great scripts with unrealistic budgets and when I tell them the truth about how much the film is going to cost they look at me like I'm lying, I'm an idiot or I hate them or their script and don't want to admit it—six months later I inquire and find out the film still hasn't been made or it was made at the budget I originally quoted them."

So you get it, right? Making friends laugh on YouTube? The under-$1,000 budget is fine. Not so fine if you want to showcase your skills at a festival with high production values, camera work, and multi-locations using professional actors.

PLEASE, NO HELICOPTER AERIAL SHOTS . . . PLEASE

On set is the time where a director needs to be both flexible and respectful of other people's time while maintaining artistic integrity. Feels impossible, but it gets done every day. Keep your creative mind *wide open* and make sure to have a professional and conscientious Director of Photography.

Initially in the script for *Dani and Alice*, 50% of the stars' dialogue was said while they were driving home from the bar. The cost of driving nixed that element of the script and as a first-time director, I really had to ask myself, "Do I actually want to ask actors to *act* such dramatic roles while they're driving the ridiculous streets of Los Angeles? WOW—look at this *fantastic* parking lot!" And it was director of photography Geary McLeod who walked me through it. Geary has worked in film and television for over twenty years. From camera assistant to director of photography, he worked on film projects such as *Lethal Weapon (1 & 2), Malcolm X, Crooklyn,* and on the television shows *Barbershop* and *Dirt.* He shares:

> "You'd be shocked at how many scripts I read that have running car shots in them. I know, when you're writing it it seems simple. You've got two people, in a confined space, talking to one another, but really ask yourself, 'Could this conversation happen over dinner?' Would it really take anything away from the story you're trying to tell? You can accomplish a lot more logistically using up way less resources if you simplify the action in your film so that we, the audience, can focus on the dialogue and characters."

Geary and I had to lose scenes, change locations, and work with a tiny budget, yet we still managed to create an award-winning film. It can be done, and you need to be *prepared* to do it. What Geary taught me (and I'm certain every other filmmaker he's worked with) is that having realistic expectations based on your budget and what the story needs will always be far easier to shoot than when you've watched too many *Starsky & Hutch* episodes. Geary continues:

> "I hate to come at it from the negative, but the first thing I look at when I read someone's script is 'What are the odds of even being able to shoot this movie?' Because it's amazing how many scripts you read that are unshootable or unshootable at the budget that this person is proposing. And what makes a script obviously unshootable to me is unrealistic shots. I remember I once read this kid's script that opened with a helicopter aerial shot. You know what?

There isn't going to be any helicopter (or moving cars, or car crashes, etc.) shots in this movie. *In a short?* A helicopter doesn't even leave the ground without thousands of dollars' worth of fuel, never mind attaching all the gear setting up a camera requires. You'd need a budget line for that one shot alone that *should* be what most short filmmakers use for their entire film."

Time to take a look at Steak and her producing partner Dominic Ottersbach's budget samples. (For the detailed formatted version of these budgets, please see page 201.)

Steak & Dominic's Budget Breakdown

$11,000 Budget (The Begging & Pleading Budget)

2-Day Weekend Shoot (weekend rates for equipment are cheaper)

35-Person Cast / Crew (all unpaid positions)

HD Camera Package w/ 35mm Lenses (record straight to hard drive)

2-ton Grip / Electric Package including Dolly

1 Cube Truck (for Grip / Electric and Camera)

1 Art Van or Fun Saver RV (this option gets you a bathroom for remote locations)

Continental Breakfast, Lunch, and Craft Service for 35 people

No Generator (Which means you have to have enough power at each location. Sometimes people won't let you plug into

continued

their outlets—sends their electric bill sky-high. Also make sure ALL of your equipment can be plugged into regular outlets. Ask your DP or Key Grip)

No Talent Trailer (set up private area for actors at each location, very important)

Free Locations, No Permits [Roberta's note: It's illegal to shoot a film without permits. While *many* filmmakers get away with it, far be it from me to suggest something illegal in this book.]

No Picture Vehicles (meaning you'll have to use your own car if the script requires your actors to be in one)

Remember: This reflects special favor rates from rental houses and a bunch of donated stuff.

$18,000 Budget (You Drive the Grip Truck Special)

Same as $11,000 Budget

Crew gets paid $100 per day (keeping in mind that this is peanuts)

Pay Casting Director $500

$32,000 Budget (Your Grandma Died 'n' Left You Some Money Budget)

Same as $18,000 Budget

3-Day Shoot

Paid Cast ($100 a day)

Filming Permits for Locations (recommended)

Generator (recommended)

Paid Locations (Don't go crazy, you can only spend $1,000)

continued

$40,000–$75,000 Budget (Oh, you're making a Hollywood movie?)

Shooting on Film: Save it for your feature.

Picture Vehicles: (Hummer to make fun of–$400/day)

Process Trailer: Plan on 5k per day. ($1,500 for the equipment, $1,000 for the driver and 2–4 cops depending on the mood of the city at $50/hr) (Gotta have a permit for this one too.)

Poor Man's Process: Actor drives the car with the DP inside or the camera on a Hostess Tray or the DP is in the back of your SUV with the back popped open and your producer holds onto her belt, so he doesn't fall out of the car.

Guns: $500 a day gets you a gun expert and for another $500 maybe he'll bring a couple guns. You *have* to get a permit if you want to fire the weapons.

A dude gets shot in the face: You'll have to make a prosthetic head for around $10k if you want it to look good, so plan on the actor getting shot on the clothes somewhere; maybe a hat?

Explosions: Your friend is a pyro and you know how to run from the law [Roberta's note: Don't even think about it.].

The last budget range ($40,000–$75,000 or over) is the one I strongly encourage you to avoid unless a) you're independently wealthy, b) you just won the lottery, or c) you have studio financing or a hefty pre-sale distribution deal (see "b").

Now, these numbers from Steak and Dominic's templates are general. Spending $23,000 on a strong, 15-page script narrative short is not unusual, but it's at this stage that I want you to get realistic about your budget. Like I always say, for creative purposes, write the script you want to write but understand that you may need to shoot a variation of that script in order to stay within budget. I had a client who took out a second mortgage on her house to finance the post on her $75,000 animation/live action *6-minute short film*. She quickly realized on the festival circuit that it was time to get another job because while her film was beautiful and accomplished it did not generate anything above praise in the press, some meetings in LA, and encouragement to keep making movies. Her huge investment may very well pay off for her eventually, but that mortgage has to get paid while she waits.

Ways to Save Money

- Get free locations. This will also keep your script simple. Everyone has access to an apartment, elevator, bedroom, or café. Just make sure you've got good people on your crew who are super-respectful of other people's stuff. You will be responsible to pay for damages when someone drags a C-stand across a hardwood floor.

- If you're not in film school, make friends with someone who is. They often have access to crew and equipment that they might be able to help you with.

- Take a community college course in editing. This way you can create your own "rough cut" to hand to an editor. This may cut your editing time in half. It will also give you time to go through your footage, giving you a clearer understanding of what you have to edit when sitting with your editor.

  (If I had known how helpful it is to understand the workings of Final Cut Pro for an indie filmmaker I would have bought it a long time ago. I did familiarize myself with it for *Happy Birthday* and was able to view all of my footage and understand what the editing process could provide me

continued

with and what was going to be impossible to fix. Get edu-
cated.)

- Don't allow your DP to decide your budget. Give him or
  her a clear and realistic budget for the camera package. If
  it's between lenses/filters or feeding your crew properly,
  go with the food. You can always add fancier elements to
  your film in post.

- Research granting organizations. There are several
  top-notch grants for filmmakers out there. Check out my
  Web site for more information: www.robertamunroe.com.

- Sell your distribution rights up-front. This is tricky because
  distributors need to know what you're capable of before
  they agree to invest. And even then it's very difficult to get
  them to give you money to make the film instead of just
  buying the rights once you're done. But, like most things
  in filmmaking, *nothing* is impossible.

- Get your producer and your post-production supervisor (if
  you don't have one yet, find someone who does) to look over
  your script *before* you shoot it. You'd be surprised at what
  can actually cost a *significant* amount of money in post.

- Take note from my students at Inner-City Filmmakers
  (www.innercityfilmmakers.com) and learn as much as you
  can about *every aspect of filmmaking.* Any one of my kids
  could light your film, shoot your film, and edit your film.
  Right now they're working with a budget of under $100,
  and once they get to the higher budget ranges they will
  have a much better understanding of how to save money.

PART 2—FINDING MONEY

Everyone thinks their short film is going to create lucrative work,
and I'm here to tell you that the chances are slim to none that

you will recoup anything over $10,000 for a short film—and that's only going to happen if your film is such a standout that it creates an income (from festivals, distribution, TV sales) or has significant lesbian, gay, transgendered content (many LGBT festivals pay rental fees for films). Most of you might—*might!*—make a few thousand in total (more about that in Chapter 9). So don't make any promises to the people who give you money to make your film about making their money back—they probably won't. Investing in filmmaking at this level isn't really investing in anything other than your talent—making *la famiglia* good people to call first.

Faced with the $5,000–$40,000 budget ranges, you say to yourself, "I don't have that kind of money nor do I know how to get it." Nonsense. You'd be surprised at how easy it is to raise it in donations, in-kind donations (where you get Kodak or Panavision to give you resources for a reduced price and you put their logo on your credit crawl), and the good old-fashioned way: Save money or get a few low-interest credit cards.

Of all the filmmakers I interviewed for this book, more than half of them self-financed on credit cards and donations from family and friends. The remainder got into film labs or made them in film school as part of their thesis project (which still cost them out of their own pocket, sometimes several thousand dollars for things film school didn't or couldn't provide). This is an important thing to make sure your family understands when you're trying to decide what distribution route to take once the film is made. You don't want to feel like you're walking the walk of shame as you enter the backyard of the next family barbecue. Orly Ravid (who we'll hear a lot more from in Chapter 9) makes a good point:

> "Filmmakers struggle to get financing for films and then also have the burden of worrying about paying their investors back so they can (a) Get that debt off their conscience and (b) Be able to tap into the same investors again. This puts a lot of pressure on the distribution of the film and

forces unrealistic or overreaching expectations of what kinds of revenues can be achieved from distribution given this competitive marketplace. But what is the case is that many films that do not make their money back can in fact propel the director's career (*e.g.*, *The Following* by Chris Nolan or *Bugcrush* by Carter Smith). I think if investors behave more like managers, they will see the long-term return from their filmmaker (and in fact an entire cast and crew). They can act like a hedge fund group—cashing in on the back-end when the filmmaker goes on to do bigger films, sells a TV show, or otherwise begins to be financially successful in their career and thus the relationship can be more of a long-term collaboration and in the short term not involve the stress of immediate payback which then strains the filmmaker's process and yields sometimes to some poor decisions to turn down viable distribution deals in search of the green cash Godot."

I PAID FOR IT MYSELF

As everyone will tell you, for a short film it is the director's job to find the money. Producers and other crew will help with donations of products and services, but when a credit card needs to get pulled out it's *always* the director's. Now, there are pros and cons to credit card–financed filmmaking. The pros are obvious, so I'm only going to discuss the cons.

You need to be clear about the kind of person you are. If you're like me, you take out $10,000 in credit only to repay almost twice that much due to the fact that (like me) you only pay the minimum payment and the interest rates keep the balance high. You cannot sleep at night (like me) because you just found out the film is going to cost another $2,000 in post-production and you're already up to your eyeballs in debt and (like me) begin to stockpile prescription sleeping pills.

Do not be like me. Only take out credit you know you can and will repay within a six-month period of time, and budget appropriately for post. Experimental filmmaker Bill Basquin (*Frank, The Odyssey, Martin, Range, The Last Day of November, The Ride*) talks about his strategy:

> "Most of my work is self-funded. I spent about $12,000 on my first film, which was 10 minutes long and shot on 16mm. I maxed out four credit cards (the limits were much lower then) and took an advance on my paycheck from work. I shoot everything on film, but since that first one, I have figured out a way to make a short film for about $5,000. This makes it easier for me to fund the films myself, and I find that I can afford to make a new film every year or two. I got a $4,500 grant for my film *Range* (this is the one that showed at Sundance) from the Film Arts Foundation, and that was great, because it almost paid for the whole film. I have now spent two years trying to raise money for my current project. I did get a grant for this one as well, but it is only a fraction of the money that I need to make the film. I have yet to delve into the world of seeking private donations, but I know that I need to. I have a 'donate' button on my Web site, but so far the only person who has made a donation is my mom (thanks, Mom!)."

THE FREE RIDE

Should you ask everyone you know with skills to work for free? Sure. My personal feelings about asking people to work for free are these: You should always be working toward having a budget where the crew are being paid at least a $100/day (keep in mind a hundred bucks a day *is* working for free for most crew members), with an increase in that number for your key people like

DP, 1st AD, and script supervisor. And don't forget that the sound person and your hair and makeup person have hard costs (batteries, kit fees), so even if you can get them to donate their time they will still need to be paid for their expendables, which can run into hundreds of dollars.

Of course, you'll probably get a few of your friends to work for free, but from what many filmmakers and producers tell me, this "free" labor isn't ever really free. First off, when people are working for free they tend to see themselves as replaceable. Maybe they show up to help out in the grip and electric department . . . maybe they don't. So now you're a crew member or two short on your already pared-down crew, and it will now take more time to set up shots . . . and what does that cost? Money.

You're thinking, Why would it cost money if I can just get a few more of my friends to work for free? Well, my dear, you have to feed people on your set. The more days you shoot, the more it costs to feed people. And no, pizza is not an option. If I've ever seen a crew walk *way* slower than they did before lunch it's after a director has bought them pizza and garlic bread for their main meal of the day. Buy them respectable food to eat and you'll get respectable results. Mark my words.

HOW DO I CONVINCE PEOPLE TO PART WITH THEIR MONEY?

You not only need to be creative, you also have to stand in the Big Belief Place.

The Big Belief Place is simple. You've read about it in magazines. You've heard filmmakers talk about it on television. Maybe you've even watched *The Secret* a few times. If you look inside you have to find the voice that says, "There is nothing I want more than to make this movie. Nothing is going to stop me from making this movie. I will make this movie regardless of how many times I hear the word 'No' or 'Never' or the phrase, 'You'll never be able to do this.'"

Leah Meyerhoff (www.leahmeyerhoff.com) is a graduate of NYU's Tisch School of the Arts, one of the best film schools in the United States. She also teaches classes there, as well as at the New York Film Academy, another really great school. She self-distributed her short film *Twitch* to over 200 festivals, where it garnered several jury and audience awards. This grand success led to her raising several hundred thousand dollars to produce her feature film *Unicorns*, which was in pre-production at the time I was writing this book. She states:

> "If you don't wake up thinking about your movie and go to sleep thinking about your movie, then you don't want it enough or the subject matter needs to be more compelling to your creative brain."

The energy you as a director put behind your creative vision comes through clearly when you talk to people about your film. It attracts the right producer, DP, actors, and *money*. It is your responsibility as the director to drive this train from point A to point B. When it comes to short films, it really is only the director who receives anything of great value from the efforts. Steak House makes this salient point:

> "When I'm producing a short I know that only the director is going to get invited to the film festival that the film gets selected for. Not me, not the DP, not the crew, and probably not even the actors unless they're highly recognizable. Directors need to keep that in mind whenever they're pitching their movie for crewing up and more importantly for financing. Financiers and crew respond to a director who has a high-energy *crystal clear* vision and is responsible and *committed* enough to see this project through to the end of post."

Melissa Bradley is the founder and CEO of New Capitalist (www.newcapitalist.com) and founder and president of Positive Impact, which is an organization that funds media makers of color in Washington, D.C. Melissa has been running the Positive Impact fund for over five years. When it comes to giving advice to filmmakers seeking funding, Melissa puts it succinctly:

> "As a funder, I look for the track record of the filmmaker, their experience/training, business acumen, vision, and credibility and I judge whether or not they can complete the project based on references I seek from their producing team, personal references and what other kinds of social capital they've been able to raise. My best advice to an up and coming filmmaker is to make sure you understand the business of filmmaking and always balance creative with financial."

It's all about you. You are the driving force and your passion has to shine like a klieg light if you want people to get on board by investing cash into your career. If you don't believe this then move on and get a job because you are going to *need* this kind of committed belief in yourself and your creative vision to work in this industry. Period.

FILM VS. DIGITAL: THE GREAT DEBATE

Financing short films is often really what would be considered "fundraising." Not everyone gets their script into a lab that underwrites the production costs, like I did with *Dani and Alice*. And even with Fox Searchlight's *foxsearchlab* behind me I still spent an additional $10,000 in cash to finish the film. I shot *Dani and Alice* on 35mm, whose budget I assumed would run a little higher than if I was shooting digitally. But shooting digitally, as I found out making *Happy Birthday*, was still a significant financial investment.

The hype we've been hearing for the past several years is that the digital era is the democratization of filmmaking. Shoot digitally and cut your budget in half! Save time and money! So I did. And the hype is that you, the filmmaker, are your own production house. The camera is portable, the stock light as air and cheap as a pack of smokes, the software is user-friendly in post-production, and you eliminate several positions that you would have needed in post if you shot on film.

Not so. Not at all. Not without a significant investment of your time *learning* the intricacies of the technology.

It was the summer of 2008 and I was standing in the kitchen of filmmaker Joshua Leonard, moaning about making DVDs for festival submissions, and he said, "Babe, all you need is an Eric Escobar in your life and all things become clear." And he's right, and I do have one very clever fount of information—Eric Escobar—in my life. Whenever Final Cut Pro began blinking its error message, *"Roberta you are a loser. If you try to 'submit' this one more time we're shutting you down. Call Eric."* (Yes, it did), I sent an SOS text message to Mr. Escobar and magically, within twenty minutes or so my problem was solved.

Filmmaker Eric Escobar (*Night Light*, Sundance 2003; *One Weekend a Month*, Sundance 2005) shares his thoughts on why you need to understand the process as you are budgeting and raising money for your movie. I talked to most people interviewed for this book in person or on the phone, but there was no way I could ask my transcriber to fully grasp on the page what Eric had to say, so I asked him to write it down. Yes, you may have to read it twice to truly understand what he's exposing. I did.

"The digital acquisition, manipulation, and distribution of the moving image has fundamentally and irreversibly changed the economics of film and media. More people are making more media, have more places to view it, while completely new types or motion picture media have taken form on the popular culture landscape (most notably user-generated short form content spread via e-mail, hosted on video sharing sites aka 'viral videos'). This is not democratization of filmmaking, it's the post-industrialization of media content creation. Films, whether studio-backed or independently-financed, and whether short or long form, were made the same way for the better part of a hundred years. An assembly line of technology and specialized skills was needed to create and disseminate content. Motion picture films required crews to build sets, hang lights and operate complicated specialized film cameras. Film post-production required labs for the chemical processing of exposed film and the synching of sound magazines. Editing was done on heavy, expensive, specialized pieces of equipment operated by highly skilled technicians.

"However, it's a mistake to think that a P2 solid state memory card has simply replaced a film magazine—it's not just a swap of the tangible for the virtual. It's a change from the fixed economics of physical assets to the constant flux of digital data. Once the technology for making films was untethered from the world of celluloid and chemicals and hitched to the electronic world, the practice and economics changed."

Until recently, I would rather have driven 45 minutes to Santa Monica, where my editor lives, than learn how to accomplish small tweaks in Final Cut Pro. It's not that I couldn't learn how to use it, it's that I chose to avoid anything that even smells like technology. I'm an artist, I cry. But as I mention in *Ways to Save Money* (pages 74–5) my students at Inner-City Filmmakers are the artists near and dear to Eric's heart. He wants us to understand the technology—from beginning to end—because it's through this understanding that you can not only be a better filmmaker, thus making a better film, BUT you can also save yourself thousands of dollars.

Eric explains how he managed to create his last short, *One Weekend a Month* (again, read it twice, this time be close to your Web browser so you can look things up):

"In 2004, I made an award-winning short film called *One Weekend a Month* shot on a professional HD broadcast camera (Panasonic Varicam). What was significant was the workflow I utilized to get the footage from the videotape to a 35mm print. Panasonic has licensed the DVCPro HD codec to Apple and designed a video cassette deck with a Firewire port in the back. This simple collaboration between two technology companies made obsolete, a half a million dollars' worth of video post-production equipment with a simple ten-dollar Firewire cable.

"I didn't have to make dubs of my HD master tapes, or spend money in an on-line suite capturing my HD footage uncompressed. I was able to 'ingest' the original quality image from the HD master tapes onto inexpensive Firewire hard drives and edit in Final Cut Pro. Once I had my locked picture, I was able to color grade in Adobe After Effects and prepare a 35mm film ready image sequence using a free plug-in from The Orphanage called eLin. Adobe has since incorporated this functionality into the latest version of their application. Production, post and film out to 35mm was about $5,000. What's most significant about this case study is that I was able to shoot and edit HD, and create a 35mm ready filmout for nothing, using off-the-shelf hardware and software. The only time there was a lab involved was in the actual transfer of my image sequence to a 35mm film negative, and the subsequent processing. People saw it screen on 35mm, DPs assumed it originated on 16mm, and audiences, even the highly educated ones at Sundance, didn't seem to care."

Using all of these inexpensive tools, a single artist, or small collective group of artists, can make a cinematic motion picture image indistinguishable from 35mm film for little to no cost. And this image can be shared instantly with a global audience. There is no need for a giant assembly line, a lab, and an army of specialized technicians. But, my friend, what it does require is that you learn as much about the computer and all its wonders as you know about writing stories and directing actors.

Get out there and find your own Eric Escobar. You will be forever grateful that you did.

WHAT NOT TO DO WHEN SHOOTING DIGITALLY

Like most filmmakers saturated with the hype, I thought shooting on HD would offer me the luxury of shooting as much as I wanted at a lower cost than shooting on 35mm. I shot on a Panasonic HVX-200 (courtesy of Trevor Hotz at www.hotcamny.com). Trevor included a small light package and two P2 cards that both had a 20-minute capacity. I thought, Wow! I can shoot all day if I want to! I shoot 20 minutes, pop that P2 card out, and while my 1st AC, Albert Oh, is downloading that card I can be shooting the next 20 minutes. And all that shooting wouldn't add anything to the overall budget because it's not rolls and rolls of film that has to get processed at the lab—the "processing" is happening on the P2 card download!

Boy, was I ever wrong.

Director of photography Geary McLeod explains why I was so wrong:

"Digital filmmaking has somewhat of a false economy to it. The one error that I see most often with filmmakers shooting digitally versus on film is that they think they don't have to be as prepared. They think, 'Oh whatever. We can just write up the shot list as we go along—it's only tape or P2 cards.' And that kind of thinking adds hundreds if not thousands of dollars to your budget."

On *Dani and Alice* I had pages of meticulously written-out shots and a complete storyboard of the script. On *Happy Birthday* I had neither of those to the extent that I did on my first film. And that cost me at least $1,000 extra to pay and feed people an extra day because we didn't get all the coverage we needed in the allotted three-day schedule.

Geary continues his point with:

"In a way, it's a good thing that with 35mm, every foot of film is precious. You don't just start shooting and hope everything works out. You have to plan your days perfectly, so you do the work required. Plus, at the end of the day, both production and post-production is still costly with digital. You *still* have to pay people on-set, you *still* have to pay an editor, and now you've got hours more footage than you'd have had with film, you *still* have to pay for a digital intermediate, you *still* have to output to something, and HD transfers do not come cheap. And then you still have to deal with sound design and mixing. And of course there is the issue of having a professional-looking film. It's possible with digital but what I tend to see a lot is people acting like they're sixteen-year-old boys who just smoked a joint and shot each other skateboarding in their backyard."

I had free locations, the HotCamNY donated Panasonic HVX-200 camera and light package, and a skeleton crew that all worked for way below their normal rate. But what I *didn't have* was enough of an understanding of what digital filmmaking was going to cost (not enough research!). In the blink of an eye (on a three-and-a-half-day shoot) I spent $2,000 on craft service and lunch, $1,000 on truck rentals and transportation (that includes the ridiculous cost of parking in New York City and the $115 parking ticket we got our *first day*), $500 on a hard drive purchase (to download the HDVX P2 cards onto), $200 on rehearsals, not to mention the $800 travel budget it cost me to go to New York to shoot. Had I done more research and done the kind of preparation I've been advising you to do, I could have saved at least a day and a half of shooting time.

And post, as Geary warns, was still just as expensive and time-consuming as when I shot on film. I had to have three editors because I had shot so much footage that I couldn't decide in a timely manner what shots to use in order to appropriately pace the film and have a good run time (the first assembly cut was a whopping 32 minutes. I wanted to kill myself for shooting so much). So the first layer was the assembly cut edit, then a rough cut edit, then a fine cut before I locked picture. Instead of the month-long process I expected, it took me several months to work it out.

Ridiculocity (my favorite made-up noun) coupled with high-end procrastination left me a few thousand dollars poorer because of all that footage. Plus all that begging I had to do with my *famiglia* to re-invest when I got to post-production since I'd gone overbudget just shooting the film (and, of course, drinking to forget my problems, in the East Village).

There are many filmmakers like Eric out there who cannot wait to try out the latest and greatest in digital technology, but I mostly found that directors and DPs say they'd rather shoot on film while producers and line producers think it's better for first-time filmmakers to shoot digitally. Which makes sense really, because film is sexy and luxurious, while digital, on the surface, seems cheap and unemotional. Film is historically the *only* way to create art in this medium—video is relegated to television, commercials, and music videos. Though I'm starting to reconsider as my hero, Mr. Sidney Lumet (whose book I tell you to read in Chapter 6) is eighty-three, a legendary director, has made over fifty feature films, and several of his latest were shot digitally.

But a really great reason to shoot digitally is that it can lessen the amount of equipment and people on set and allow you to focus your energies on more important things—like, let's say, performances. Filmmaker Madeleine Olnek (*Hold-Up, Make Room for Phyllis, Countertransference*), a firm believer in shooting digitally, makes the great point about focusing on story versus on high-budget technology:

> "As a director, you have to decide what are the most important things to you—literally, what are you going to place a value on. Shooting format can partially determine that, especially in the limited fund-raising world of shorts. Equipment-wise too, sometimes placing a value on one thing means placing less of a value on something else. If you have a gigantic crane shot and a cube truck that you are negotiating the operation of, are you really going to have any space of your brain left to pay attention to the nuances of your actors' performances? Personally, I think story and performances are the most important thing, and I always try to shoot in a cheap format (usually 24p), so that everyone's attention is on creating magic with the actors rather than on gigantic load-ins, equipment operation, etc. I try to spend a lot of money on really good food so that people feel appreciated and work well. Hollywood blockbusters do the big-production value thing the best; people are drawn to watching shorts because of the very exciting and unusual stories that can be told in the short film format. I think it makes the most sense, if you are going to be making a short, to put your attention and resources into the acting and the story."

So let's just say, if you're shooting a one-note joke in your kitchen, video/digital may be the most economical route. If you're shooting a fifteen-page dramatic narrative that you want to win Best Short at some top-tier film festival or win an Academy Award, you would be wise to seek to raise enough of a budget to at least *consider* shooting on film or have the capability to output your digital work to film.

Be smart. Be prepared, regardless of what format you choose to shoot on.

WHERE DO I BEGIN THE SHAKEDOWN?

Should you organize a car wash? Yes. Should you call your ex-boyfriends, ex-girlfriends, aunts, uncles, cousins, and grand-parents to contribute $10–$1,000 to your production? Yes. Many smart filmmakers I know, like the unstoppable Erin Greenwell (*Big Dreams in Little Hope, Commitment Ceremony, Overnight Book*) signed up at www.justgive.org. They offer a wonderful service where people can donate to your project and receive a tax deductible receipt, provided that you are a registered not-for-profit, with 501(c)(3) status with the IRS. Go online and do some research.

GET THE WORD OUT THAT YOU NEED MONEY

I know filmmakers who sent a general request to their entire e-mail list. In order to do this you'll need to find a fiscal sponsor whose not-for-profit status would qualify your project. There are some great ones like IFP and Women Make Movies (both in New York City)—go online and do some research.

The request was simple: Please contribute to my short film. They posted a synopsis of the script, who was producing, who they'd cast (with photos!) and what their intention was (e.g., "I want to capture the universal terror we all feel leaving a voice-mail message"). They created their own financing community and they held strong to the Big Belief.

Make it easy for people to contribute, set up an online account (like PayPal), add a "Donate Now" button to your Web site, and watch the dollars flow. There are also several not-for-profit organizations that can act as a fiscal sponsor for your project that you may qualify for depending on your script and the size of your budget. A fiscal sponsor essentially funnels cash donations, which is a win-win situation. The donor receives a tax deduction, you receive much-needed funds, and the fiscal sponsor receives a small percentage (generally around 3–8%) for their hard work. Please go on my Web site, www.robertamunroe.com, for more information.

And, finally, remember: Filmmaking has to be one of the most expensive creative mediums *ever*. Whether you shoot digitally or on film, be honorable with other people's money. They are really investing in your career, in *you*—they will not get back the money they invest in your short film. Take care of their investment, make a great short, and maybe they'll be even more generous when you move on to features.

5

Crewing Up

Once you have a producer who's there to oversee the production of your film, you move on to the other key players. As I noted earlier, many times producers will have people they often work with who fill the various roles below the line crew. Hiring these people is a little tricky, because they are often beholden to the producer and not you. The producer works on many films and is able to gainfully employ them throughout the year. You, on the other hand, are only going to be working on one project at a time. Be aware of this fact when discussing your creative vision with key crew members and make sure your producer is backing you up on your vision.

Something else filmmakers rarely think about are *group dynamics*. When it comes to a film set you have to factor this in. I know, you're thinking, "What is she talking about?! I'm just making a movie!" But you're still making that movie with *human beings*. I reached out to Agape practitioner Monica Guevara, who not only holds a PhD in corporate psychology, but group dynamics are her life's passion. Whenever I have to go to a meeting where there will be more than three people I call her, give her each person's stats, and she gives me an outline of how to handle my stuff within the group. Monica is also a huge movie fan who came on board not to just donate but also to staff our craft service table during the *Dani and Alice* shoot. She was happy to share her thoughts around the group dynamics on a film set:

> "Remember everyone has their perspective and their history, so their reality may be quite different from yours—there are many stories going on at the same time. Your job is to be as clear about yours so they can help you—*without* invalidating their uniqueness. Always show how people's uniqueness is valuable and helpful in creating something. That is why they are in those jobs to begin with. Also remember that a group has a personality of its own which is why each film crew has a different feel. Try to figure out what kind of personality that group has. You are a leader as well as a director. You are counted on for a respectful vision and direction (literally).
>
> "And, know that EVERY group goes through a period of 'jelling,' so don't freak out if things get rocky. People need to learn each other, let off steam as they're learning—just make sure their direction continues to be forward and positive. Use your other key crew [producers are usually good in this role] to deal with problems if you need to. Keep your vision clear. Know what is yours, theirs, and yours together. Some things are really none of your business and don't have to be tolerated or dealt with on the set. OWN your stuff. You will stand out as a great director and you will keep people from sabotaging you and giving you a bad reputation. Take time to work things out with others if you need to—that time you take may very well save you even more time down the road."

WHO NOT TO MAKE A MOVE WITHOUT
CONSULTING FIRST

Post-Production Supervisor

Before I even shoot? A good post supervisor will be able to walk you through the treacherous waters of post *before* you start shooting. My friend, I could fill an entire book on the post of *Dani and Alice* because I didn't have a post supervisor and had no idea how intricate the details of post were. And they *are* intricate whether you're shooting on film or digitally. Find someone who has done post many times on the format you're shooting. Ask them to walk you through the various possibilities of finishing your film. And they are indeed various, my friend. Shoot on 16mm, blow up to 35mm or output to HD. Shoot digitally, have animated sections, green screen shots, and want to output to film. Shoot on 35mm and output to HD. Shooting on HD but editing with a 29.97 frame rate instead of 24. The variations are endless. But if you listen carefully you will learn what options there are and how much they cost and how long they will take to achieve.

Remember way back to Chapter 2, how you're supposed to know everything there is to know about your story? Now you can have a professional post supervisor help you with the technical aspects so you can achieve your goals.

A good post supervisor will:

- Be patient and clear.
- Provide you with information in language *you* can understand.
- Point out all of your options with clarity about what they cost.
- Tell you the truth in terms of what can and may go wrong within the structure of shooting and post you eventually choose (because, darling, things *will* go wrong and it's better to know about them up front).

Editor

What? Another post person before I even start shooting my movie? Look, you think you know exactly how this film will look once you're done with the script, but an editor can help you (along with your DP) refine your shot list before you start production. You will be sad when you get into the edit and he or she says, "Sorry, you can't do that, you don't have that coverage" or "Yeah, I tried to do that but the shots don't match up."

My editor on both my shorts, Paul Heiman, told me he always gives filmmakers what he calls the Rough Cut Speech (more on this later, in Chapter 8). It's a gentle reminder that just in case you may not have everything, he has come up with solutions to help you tell your story. You want to work with someone like Paul, a truly talented editor who wants to help you get the best film possible, not just get you out the door because you're not paying him or her the union scale rate of $2,800 a week.

A good editor will:

- Give you options and not try to make *you* take the easiest road in order to make *their* job easier, regardless of how much you're paying them—they go the extra distance.
- Be creative when you don't have the coverage truly helping you tell your story with the footage you have.
- Be honest with you about how much time they have to spend on your film (so you don't freak out that it's taking twice as long as you thought it would).
- Help you get to a difficult decision *without* making that decision for you without your input.

Keep in mind that your editor is really another wonderful, creative second pair of eyes on your masterpiece. (Go out right now and buy Walter Murch's book *In the Blink of an Eye*. He's a celebrated film editor who has written a concise and accessible book.) It is in the edit that most films are created for the second time. And your responsibility as a director is to treat your editor like a creative partner. This isn't just about being nice and showing up with dinner (though I'm sure they'd appreciate your efforts) but it's also about realizing that a really good editor has worked on a number of films before yours. They have insights, experience, and know-how that you do not at this stage in your career and they are able to see things that work and don't work long before you are.

Director of Photography/Cinematographer

The DP is your best friend on your shoot. And he or she is the person who can be a leader in making your shoot run beautifully, or create such chaos that every new setup is like getting a root canal.

As I said earlier, Geary McLeod was a dream to work with because, well, because he's a bloody genius. He and I had done such great prep work (which he essentially taught me in pre-production how to accomplish) that he understood exactly the look I was going for, had great respect for the actors and their contribution, and was instrumental in our having a top notch Key Grip, Gaffer, and camera crew.

Geary made sure I was prepared. He insisted on a "look book" (which is a book you, the director, create with colors, images, and tones that you'd like your film to have. I used magazines, tearing out photos that had elements of what I was looking for visually and tonally). And he also insisted on a completely-thought-through shot list, which was invaluable once we started having to lose shots due to time constraints. I already knew which ones were the ones that could get thrown out.

Now, I've been on shoots where the DP is crazy disorganized, screams at the crew, has contempt for the actors, ignores your requests for changes, and the worst—thinks they know better than you how the film should be directed. This is a DP who really wants to be a director, and you want to stay as far away from this person as possible.

Zachary Adler (*Familiar Strangers, I'm Reed Fish, Something in Between, Late*) discusses a nightmare moment:

> "I worked with one DP on one of my films where the relationship was tumultuous. He was a true artist, talented *and* tortured. The scariest and funniest moment was when he threw the Panasonic 35mm camera *at* me after threatening to throw it in the ocean. He then jumped on, and began punching, the boom operator."

Remember—interview your potential crew AND get references.

Also, be mindful to take a good look at their reels. Do they use the camera in a way that resounds with what you want your film to look like? Do they do a great job with 35mm but all their video/digital work looks over- or under-lit? Does the camera never stop moving, distracting you from the story? Is there a dolly-push shot when a push would do? Do you even need a push in this scene? Are you choosing a DP who is able to be super-creative when you simply don't have thousands of dollars for gels and duvatine or will they go over budget to <u>get the shot?</u>

And please, do not offer carrots to get a DP on board. Your producer will be pissed if you make promises to get a cinematographer, particularly promises that cost significant amounts of money, which is pretty much everything a DP uses. When the sauce hits the fan and you have to go back on promises made, you may find yourself looking for a new last-minute DP.

As with anything in life, hiring people (for pay or not) to do a job you have already envisioned as a final product can be tricky. Carter Smith talks about how to let go without letting go of your vision by being super-prepared:

"It was my dream for so long and it felt so freeing to be able to hand the camera over to my director of photography Darren Lew. The moment that I got on set I felt like I was at home. The night before of course I was so nervous I could barely sleep but the moment I got on set I felt over prepared and confident. My storyboards were done, shot list done, *Directing Actors* [by Judith Weston] read, scene breakdown done, which for my thirty-six-page script took weeks and whenever I got stuck I would reread Judith's book and move forward."

Filmmaker Danielle Lurie (*In the Morning*, Sundance 2005) found her director of photography while watching another film-maker's movie. (Exactly why I say *get out there* and watch stuff!) She comments:

"The best thing that came out of production was my falling creatively in love with my cinematographer. Never before had I known the joys of creative collaboration like this. An-drew Huebscher had shot my friend's short the year before, and when I decided to make *In the Morning*, I called Andrew before I had even written the screenplay to ask him to shoot my film. He was the first person on board—even before my producer. We began discussing the look of the film about a year before we shot it, constantly exchanging ideas and film references and by the time we were rolling cameras our film was looking exactly as I had envisioned it—even better than I could have imagined it actually—thanks to Andrew!"

1st AD (Assistant Director)

The favorite line a 1st AD likes to shout is, "Moving on!" This means you have made your shot and the crew is to *move on* to begin the next setup for your next scene. While you and your DP are hiding behind a parked car trying to figure out how to set up the next shot as quickly as possible, the 1st AD is hunting you down to *help you* so you have time to make that next shot. She knows everything there is to know about the shooting schedule of your film because she created it. Make friends with your 1st AD! She is there to help guide your shoot in a way no one else can. You'll be a better director for the connection. Carter Smith explains how having a great 1st AD on *Bugcrush* meant so much for the success of his film:

> "I had two different 1st ADs. We shot six days then we shot another two days. I really think if I'd had the second 1st AD initially we would have been able to get it all shot in those first six days. My advice to every filmmaker is make cuts elsewhere in order to hire a top-notch 1st AD who you pay a good rate to. A 1st AD is not there for any other reason than for you to make your day of shooting. They're not getting shots for their reel or worried about banking credits."

And director of photography Alison Kelly, who has been the cinematographer on more than twenty short films and several features, notes:

> "I think one of the biggest mistakes I've seen on first-time director shorts is not recognizing that every position exists for a really good reason, and thinking that you can combine stuff or thinking that you don't need, like, a production designer, for example. And usually they don't understand what the 1st AD does, and they hire a girlfriend or a best friend to just sort of keep it on schedule. They feel like all they need to do is just hold a watch and keep a schedule. It couldn't be farther from the truth—that is the antithesis of what the 1st AD should be doing. The 1st AD should be such a fundamental part of that creative team that they're inseparable from those creative conversations. They are

integral on set. That person is my best friend; I love a good AD. They make it all possible. One of the most important things for me is to be involved with the scheduling. You really want your DP, the 1st AD, and yourself to sit down at least a week beforehand, and talk through the schedule, look at each day in detail, try and figure out what are the red flags—this scene is going to take long because it's in a car, or whatever it is. I've seen directors have a total meltdown because this wasn't taken care of and subsequently made it a very uncomfortable experience for everyone else."

WHO DOES WHAT

Line Producer/Production Manager

Unless you have a bunch of money to make your short, you usually have one or the other to do both jobs. This is the right-hand person who handles the budget and all things (outside of talent, your DP, and their crew) necessary for production. Things like managing the budget (set out by the producers—and your credit card limit), talent transportation, production drivers, SAG and extras paperwork, PAs (production assistants), catering, and craft service personnel. They work in close conjunction with the 1st AD, who is in charge of making sure your shoot stays on schedule. Most times on short film shoots this person is almost always also one of the producers (or *the* producer) on the film.

What a number of successful filmmakers I know have done is to seek out people who are coming up through the producing ranks as line producers. The awesome thing about hiring a line producer to be your producer is that they have a solid understanding of how much things cost and what you can replace with cheaper but as effective replacements. You and your DP want hundreds of dollars' worth of gels and your line producer knows a place that will give you a few pieces of critical used gels for free. You need to cover a bunch of windows on a location and they know where to grab used (and *free*) duvatine. They have built relationships with filmmaker resources centers like Filmmakers Alliance and IFP and companies like Color by Deluxe, FotoKem, or Kodak that you will greatly benefit from.

Gaffer and Key Grip

As for as the camera crew, your Gaffer (person who physically lights the film according to the DP's specifications) and the Key Grip and their grip and electric team (people who work closely with Gaffer and DP running cables, setting up lights, operating dollies, etc.) are all the domain of your DP. You are rarely talking directly to these people (except maybe chatting at dinner break or thanking them for a job well done—which you *should* go out of your way to do as often as possible), and if you are, you didn't hire the right DP or you're a megalomaniac.

Script Supervisor/Continuity

The Script Supervisor is the person who sits beside the director documenting each and every take. They will also act as a second pair of eyes for continuity in each take. They make notes based on what the director says: "I like that one," "She missed her mark," and so on. They might lean over and say, "Julie had her hand on Yolonda's thigh when she said her line in the last take and on this take she didn't." They are there because *you are never going to remember* which take you liked and which you didn't. They are there because you *are never going to notice* something as small as a hand on a thigh. On small shoots people tend to forget about the Scripty. Why they're important: If you get into your edit and cannot remember which shot of the nine takes you really liked and now you're wasting valuable time with your editor looking for it . . . you needed a Script Supervisor. If you get into your edit and realize your actor says one line four different ways, doing four different things with his body, looking in four different directions . . . you needed a Script Supervisor. If you shot on film and the picture and sound slates don't match . . . you needed a Script Supervisor. (And if you need further evidence of how important they are, Wikipedia has a *full page* dedicated to what a Script Supervisor is responsible for, on-set and off.)

Production Designer/Art Director

Again, here's a position that gets forgotten on many shorts. Why it's important: If I'm watching your film and all I notice is the mismatched avant-garde paintings on the wall behind the actors who are making loud passionate love . . . you needed a Production Designer. If I'm watching your film and in one scene there is a huge bouquet of flowers on the table and when we cut back to it it's disappeared, because a grip moved it during lunch and forgot to put it back and you are too busy to remember it was there originally, you needed a Production Designer. But most importantly, they can be *invaluable* when it comes to helping you set a visual tone to your film. Do your best to get one on board.

Hair, Makeup Artists, and Costume Designer

Most hair people can do makeup and vice versa, which can save you money, but not all of them do both, so make sure to ask. However, if you know you'll need a significant amount of either necessary before you can roll camera, hire two separate people, otherwise it'll take forever to get your actors on set. If you think you can just get your friend who's pretty good with her own hair, makeup, and wardrobe, think again. Why it's important to hire professionals: If I'm watching your film and at the beginning of the scene the actor is wearing a sleeveless dress and when we cut back to her she's put a sweater over it—you needed a Costume Designer (on shorts it's often simply called Wardrobe). If I'm watching your movie and the female actor who has just finished making that passionate love (noted above) looks like she's ready for a photo shoot—springy curls, glossy lipstick, and all—you needed a Makeup and Hair person.

GENIUS SURROUND

It should be clear to you by now that how good your film will be is based solely on how good of a team you've surrounded yourself with. I call this "genius surround." Of course things will go wrong, but if you surround yourself with *genius*, things will go a lot smoother.

All the DPs I spoke to for this book always said at some point in the interview that when they first meet with the director they also always evaluated the rest of the team with the same detail. Sure the script is great, the director seems to have a clear vision, but who is producing the film? Who will be their 1st AD? Their editor? Script Supervisor? What kind of support does this director have to realize her vision? Alison Kelly notes:

> "Especially with first-time directors, a lot of times there are so many ideas about what the director should and should not behave like and be like on set. And a lot of people, I think, feel an incredible amount of maybe not performance anxiety, but just this *expectation* of what they should be doing. And worse, that they should *know* everything, and that there shouldn't be any pausing or discussion of things, so that when the 1st AD says, 'What's up next?' they should always be able to say what's up next, and they should always have *all* the answers for the actors, and there's a lot of stress that goes into that experience. But I think it's important to have people on your team—the DP, the producer, and hopefully a production designer who a) aren't putting that stress on you, and b) are allowing you the creative space to feel comfortable, to not feel like you need to have *all* the answers.

The best gift you can give somebody is to make that creative space for them."

I echo that sentiment. I can't say it enough—surround yourself with people who know more than you do and are committed to working on your project with everything they've got . . . whether you're paying them their full rate or they're working for lunch and gas money. At the end of the day it will be you, the director, who will have to stand in front of an audience. It will be you, the director, who receives all those blasted rejection letters because you thought you could do it all yourself, or because you hired people you could feel in your gut were not the best person for the job. You cannot do it all yourself—no one can. And if anyone tells you differently—they're lying.

6

Casting Talent

You know your script is great because you did everything I told you to do in Chapter 1 and now you're ready to hire those amazing people who are going to bring your carefully crafted characters to life!

Adrienne Weiss is a great acting coach and film director in her own right who facilitates workshops for directors (www .directingactors.com). Her practical and craft-based approach offers directors, screenwriters, and actors concrete tools to marry their imagination and intuition with the archetypes of dramatic storytelling. Adrienne has directed several features including *Love, Ludlow* (Sundance 2005), and has coached several renowned actors including Paul Giamatti, Joan Cusack, and Lili Taylor. She shares her wisdom:

> "I learned, when I was teaching at NYU, that one of the things people compromised on was who they cast. I feel like it's one of those key things that really makes a short work—you have a really special performer in there, an actor who has a real quality that makes you interested

cinematically. *Especially* in a short. You don't have the time to really get to know a person, so you have to see them and get a feeling. I feel like a lot of times people just end up settling, and then the whole movie, you're just setting the level of what you can achieve lower, from the get-go, if you choose that. So one of the things I said to people a lot at NYU was 'don't settle.' Keep looking. I really think if you say, 'I'm not going to compromise. I'm going to wait until I find someone who really excites me, who really has the best qualities,' you *will* find them."

Some filmmakers go online using a casting Web site where you can both post your script and peruse the thousands of actors listed. Some put out the word to fellow filmmakers or actor friends. I mean, what's the worst thing that could happen? Danielle Lurie (*In the Morning*) answers that question for us:

"My short is a drama about the practice of 'honor killings'— where a woman who commits any form of disobedience (usually in the form of adultery) can be killed by a member of her own family in a culturally sanctioned murder. Because my film's total budget was five thousand dollars, we had no real money for casting—and I cast my film by placing a twenty-dollar ad in *Backstage West* where I called all Turkish actors in Los Angeles to come read for various roles in a 'Turkish familial drama.' I got flooded with head shots from every Turk in LA—and was blown away by the ones who actually came in to audition. All was going great—until I told the actors what the film was about (until then they had just read a few disjointed scenes of sides). When they learned it was about 'honor killings,' every single Turkish actor walked out of the audition room. They all did this for one of two reasons: 1) this sort of thing doesn't happen in their country and I don't know what I am talking about or 2) this sort of thing does happen, but it's none of my business as an American director to tell this story. Regardless, they weren't doing my film, and I suddenly had no Turkish actors to play an all-Turkish family whose dialogue was all Turkish."

Which leads me to suggest . . .

HIRE A CASTING DIRECTOR

Why would you hire a casting director? It's simple. Just like you have a producer to be the person who deals with the crew and the vendors, your casting director can act as a buffer between you and the hiring of the actors. They've done this on a hundred films—they simply know more than you do. So many directors I know think, "Oh, no one is going to want to work with me. This is my first short and I should be prepared to go it alone." That's nonsense—you'd be surprised, with the right script and the right attitude, exactly how many people you can get on board with your project. Matthew (Matt) Lessall is a freelance casting director based in Los Angeles. He's been nominated for three Artios Awards and has cast many, *many* shorts that have appeared at festivals all over the world as well as more than thirty feature films including *Mean Creek* (Sundance 2004) and *Rocket Science* (Sundance 2007) (www.lessallcasting.com). He concurs:

"There are a couple of reasons to hire a casting director. One, is you want to see if you can get some sort of recognizable face into the film, and two, because you want to establish a relationship with the casting director. Though, you have to have reasonable expectations of what the casting director's going to do, because most likely you're not paying for their services. You might not get Amy Kaufman, but you might get her assistant. It just depends on how busy that individual casting director is. If you go to the casting director Web site, there's a place to go look at casting directors and mention that you're making a short film. The other way to do it is find a casting director that you really like, and say, 'I think you're right for this film.' Call up or e-mail. I've done a lot of short films and I've worked with all different budgets, and once I say, 'Yes I'll help cast your film,' the process doesn't change just because the budget is small. All you need to understand is that if the budget is limited, my time working on it and the people you may find who are interested to be involved as actors may also be limited."

A good casting director:

- Doesn't tell you she can get Halle Berry for your short.
- Keeps her appointments with you.
- Provides you with as many options as possible.
- Is prepared for every audition.
- Never lets you settle.

Something else to remember when deciding to hire a casting director is that they have access to the larger management and talent agencies. Managers and agents, like every other group that works in film, always have up-and-coming actors as clients, people they'd like to get as much exposure as possible. If your script has juicy characters written in it they might help you out. Plus, if you have a casting director shopping your script around *you as a director* also get on the radar of these agencies. Not a bad thing to have happen, my friend. Talent agent Craig Kestel (William Morris Agency) agrees:

"I find most casting directors are receptive to helping filmmakers on their short films and their first features, but it always comes down to the material. There are a few casting directors that navigate these waters pretty well, and I've reached out to them a few times since they have always managed to get the filmmakers I work with some pretty impressive results."

Some people have access to established casting directors who are willing to help cast short films as a way to meet actors and keep their skills sharpened. As I noted earlier, with *Dani and Alice*, I was blessed to be invited into the Fox Searchlight Directors Lab, *foxsearchlab*, and one of the perks of being in that lab was having the über-talented Matt Lessall cast my film. Matt talks about having realistic expectations in casting a short film:

"More often than not, the director already has someone in mind for their movie. And, unfortunately, more often than not that someone they have in mind is Halle Berry. They've got a tiny budget and this is their first film but they're *certain* if she could just read the script she would say yes. Now, some directors want to know the truth up front. They want to hear from me that there is no way Ms. Berry is going to say yes to their indie short. They want to see the list of truly talented actors who would say yes or at the very least meet with them to discuss the role. But there are always those directors, whom you know by the way they talk about their script, that they do not want to hear the truth. It's the worst thing for a casting director. And if a casting director leads you to believe that they can get Halle Berry for your short film, they're lying."

Though Ms. Berry would have been lovely, I knew I was going to use Yolonda Ross (Alice) and Guinevere Turner (Alice's best friend, Olivia), but I still needed my Dani and my Nick (Dani's best friend) and Matt was instrumental in finding Lisa Branch and Linda Husser.

And Matt warns us against just hiring a casting director because they're free—do your research:

"How much do you pay a casting director for a short film? Well, I guess it all depends on the overall budget of the short. I have a minimum fee that I charge. I have come to determine over time, what is involved in casting a short. Most of the time it depends on how busy I am. If you catch me in a slow period I may be more willing to do the short for less money. If I love the script and the director, I will probably do the short, but never for free. I know some casting directors will work for free. You have to look for what works for you. Though there is that saying, 'If you pay peanuts, you get monkeys.' Don't get stuck with monkeys—your film will suck."

I sat in the casting room with the always outstanding Effie T. Brown, while Matt Lessall read with several actors. The task: Find a beautiful talented Black actress who can and will play a lesbian who beats up her girlfriend. No easy feat, but with a great casting director this was accomplished in less than two weeks!

Many filmmakers I spoke with agreed life was easier with a casting director. Abigail Severance discusses her process:

"I've cast films both with and without a casting director, and I think there are both benefits and drawbacks. Using one is immensely helpful if they are good at their job. It's rare that we tiny filmmakers have a good enough budget for a good casting director, but it does save you a tremendous amount of time. My casting director on *Saint Henry*, Robert McGee, was fantastic not only because he got access to actors that I couldn't reach, and did all the preliminary legwork for me, but also because he has a great eye for the unusual, the underground, the quirky parts of an actor. I wouldn't have chosen Max Van Ville to play Twiggy without Robert's input because I thought he was too jittery and too odd, and he turned in one of the best performances in the film."

Carter Smith had a similar experience when casting *Bugcrush*:

"Donald [Cumming] wasn't an actor. He had no formal training but he had worked with casting director Jennifer Venditti in past commercial shoots. She knew it was him. I still wasn't convinced. It took a friend, someone who was removed from the process entirely, to help me see that Josh and Donald were electric on screen together. I'd cast Josh first so when I showed my friend the videotape from their audition together, he told me point blank, 'You would be stupid not to hire Donald.' They were both right. Donald's performance was something everyone who saw the film and many festival programmers talked about. Both he and Josh [Barclay Caras] were amazing to work with."

THE AUDITION

Be patient and understand the differences between a **good audition,** a **bad audition,** and a **nervous audition.** Always listen to your gut and the instincts of the highly qualified people you've chosen to help you (namely, your producer and casting director).

The first type of audition is when, without the pressure of film rolling, an actor is able to bring solid skills to the table that *may or may not* happen once they're on set. The second is when the actor does not give a performance that rings true to your vision. The third is the very tricky one—this is the one where the actor you feel in your gut is *the person* who is going to create the character you've been dreaming of but is nervous in the room and gives a rather lackluster performance. Also keep your eyes peeled for the actor who comes in to audition for one role but you know would be perfect for another. Thank her and politely ask her to read for the other character. Again, keep that creative brain wide open. Remember, these are the people who are going to inspire your written word with compelling action. If you do not spend the pertinent amount of energy getting the best talent your film is doomed.

I got very lucky in *Dani and Alice*. Lisa Branch (who played Dani) nailed the audition and nailed the actual performance in the film itself. And once on set we rarely had to do a retake because of her. The same for Yolonda Ross (who played Alice). And on *Happy Birthday*, my second short that starred Julie Goldman, Deak Evgenikos and I brought back, in very different roles, both Yolonda and Lisa. I would often find myself turning to my producer, Marina Guzman, to say, "Wow, Yolonda is such a great actor! Man, Lisa was amazing in that take! Or Deak (Evgenikos) is a one-take wonder!" Or, "Julie Goldman is a rock star!"

These are the kind of actors you want to suss out in auditions: performers like Lisa, Yolonda, Deak, and Julie. Actors who not only embody the characters you've written, but who are also professionals, great listeners, and the kind of performers who take nothing personally.

Some directors and casting directors will set up a video camera to tape the auditions. I did this, but to be honest I don't think I ever looked at those tapes afterwards. I always went with my gut. Abigail Severance explains her process:

> "In the casting room, it's crucial to be respectful and open with your actors. If you do *anything* to intimidate them, you will not see their best performance. I find that the more I can put them at ease—usually by highlighting my own

foibles—the more they will show me. Like most relationships, if I put out for them, they will put out for me. Also, I
think it's vital to not videotape the first round of auditions. If
you can't remember performances that you saw that day,
then they don't deserve to be in your movie. I make notes in
the first auditions, and only videotape callbacks, when I
have two actors reading together and I might miss something one actor is doing because I'm watching the other
one."

DO YOUR RESEARCH

As I mentioned earlier, Adrienne Weiss holds directing actors
workshops, but presently she only does them in New York and
Los Angeles (Adrienne is working on a book—so keep an eye out
for it). However, there are other directing coaches who provide
workshops in many cities, big and small. If you seek, you shall
find. And if you can't afford workshops or coaches then—go out
and buy Judith Weston's *Acting for Directors*. It's a start. It's a
great start. It's a great book that outlines more questions, provides more direction and insight into acting than I could possibly cover in this chapter. Almost every successful filmmaker I've
spoken with has read her book, whether they went to film school
or not. And the other book I always read before shooting is
Sidney Lumet's *Making Movies*—it's a classic.

NAW, WE DON'T NEED TO REHEARSE IT TOO MUCH

You will be sad if you don't take the time not only to develop a
solid relationship between you and your actors but to allow them
to relate to each other as well. Adrienne Weiss comments:

"Another common thing I hear people say a lot is, 'I should
have rehearsed more.' It's incredible. So many directors get

so caught up in the demands of production they forget about rehearsing with their actors. I see feature filmmakers do this all the time too; it's so easy to get all caught up. The *one* thing that only *you* can do is get the actors prepared. So it's imperative that you make that plan. So much of what's on screen is a sense of relationship between characters. A deep, subtextual relationship where you see two people sitting at a table, and you can say, 'I get it. I see it.' And actually, one of the most common things that make up lackluster perfor-mances is a lack of relationship between the actors. It's not that hard to get it, but you have to know how to get it and take a little time to do it. One of the things you can do is re-ally bond with your actors, get them really comfortable with you, do lots of improv, so that they can live together and have experiences and have a common language. There are other things you can do, such as communicating to your ac-tors one character's point of view on the other, and the other character's point of view on them, and then bingo, you have a relationship."

I had the opportunity to sit in on one of Adrienne's classes in New York and in between moments I got to ask the actors their thoughts on working with first-time or short-film directors. And one of her students, Katie Wallack, concurs on the rehearsal as-pect of filmmaking:

"You know, I used to think it was such a waste of time that in the beginning of rehearsals people were just sitting around chatting. I thought we should all just be getting straight to work! But I realized that what we're actually doing during that time is creating a rapport, a trust, and that carries us through the production. I liken it to the corporate world, that's why those people have 'business dinners' to develop a relationship *before* they start working together."

Acting is a job. A fun, creative, exciting, and very rewarding job. Just as filmmaking is a creative business, so is acting. Find people for whom this is true. Yes, there will be moments when you think to yourself, "Wow, these people should hate me—they are actually being damaged as human beings by the difficult script I am asking them to perform! What is wrong with me?" Slow down, take a breath, and just maybe you'll get some insight into the process of acting the way Danielle Lurie did on *In the Morning*:

> "We'd just filmed a truly horrific rape scene, and I had never felt so terrible. The scene was so graphic that I knew the actors really must have felt like they were actually in that reality, and an enormous sense of guilt came over me that I had put two people in such a compromising situation. I felt dirty and disgusting for having made a woman get a very good sense of what it must feel like to have been raped, and for having made a man feel the evil of being a rapist. I remember I just sat in my chair by myself as the crew packed up in the distance, feeling sick to my stomach at having just put everyone through that horrid experience. I was in a somber daze questioning whether this whole thing was worth it when my two actors—the ones who had just done the rape scene together—both came up to me with big smiles on their faces.
>
> "'Thanks for having us do that,' the actress, Anais, said.
>
> "'Yeah—that was one of the best acting experiences of my life,' came from Ludwig, the actor.
>
> "'Really?' I said.
>
> "Anais replied, 'I mean, it was really hard, but I am really glad to have done it.'"

One of my personal struggles while working with actors is the overwhelming desire to give an actor a "line-reading." A line-reading is when I *say* the line from the script in the *manner or tone* I want the actor to say it because they're not saying it the way I think it should be said. They hate that; I hate feeling so out of options that I have to do that; and, truly, it rarely brings the results I'm seeking. I wrote the script, I mapped out the entire film, and one of the things I also did was *repeatedly,* hundreds of times by this point in the process, *hear* the words being said in a specific way. I took the opportunity to ask acting/directing coach Adrienne Weiss to fill us in on some techniques to help smooth the path:

> "Usually, what the problem is, is that you want them to say it in a certain *tone*. And they're not saying it in that tone, so it feels like, 'The only way I can get them to say the line with the tone is to say it,' so they get it nonverbally almost. It's transmitted to them without you describing it in other words. Say something like, 'I can't live without you' instead of 'Don't leave me.' You can communicate the emotional tone by paraphrasing the words. The problem with a line-reading is, if they hear those words in the tone you want them, they then don't *own* those words personally. One of the techniques I use I call the 'bad friend director.' For example, when you're having a conflict a good friend will help you gain perspective on it, calm you down, not get you more agitated. A bad friend goes, 'Yeah, he is an asshole. You should send an angry e-mail.' They will encourage your agitation, your anger, your foolish desires. In life, you want to avoid that. But when you're directing, it's a very positive thing to be a bad friend."

Everyone worth their salt wants to expand (not contract) in their work. Whether your film is a comedy, intense drama, or experimental can offer actors the opportunity to do just that. Don't be afraid to push limits, just be supremely selective with whom you choose to explore those limits.

DIRECTING ACTORS

Now, there are walls, literally, *walls* of books on how to direct actors in every major bookstore. I wouldn't dream of trying to condense an entire library of information into a paragraph, but there are some tricks to the trade. Adrienne gives us one:

"The most important shift to make when preparing to direct your actors is to move from an intellectual or 'literary' understanding of what your characters are going through towards direction that is going to activate your actors into actually having that experience in front of the camera. In other words, you want to move away from result-oriented direction ('More happy! More sad!') and instead start thinking about what the facts are in your character's life that are MAKING them angry, or MAKING them sad. Here's an example: Let's say your character hates their job because of an abusive boss, and your story is about how, after taking that abuse for a long time, your character finally rebels. You're getting ready to shoot the big scene where your character tells the boss off, but you feel your actor is not sufficiently angry. The temptation is to say, 'No. You're really pissed off here. REALLY pissed off!' or something along those lines. The result of this will either be a) that your actor stares at you blankly, beginning to get pissed off at *you* for giving them result direction, or b) (most likely), that they will dutifully follow your direction and what you will get on screen will be a very generic performance of 'pissed off-ness' instead of an actual character in an actual situation. Alternatively, it would be a lot more effective to sidle up to your actor and say quietly: 'You know what I overheard him (the boss) say last night? He laughed and said that you were a wimp who would never stand up for himself. He said he'd known rabbits that had shown more spunk! And now he's asking you to work on Christmas Day, when you know damn well that if he hadn't been so disorganized that this could have been done weeks ago! What are you going to do about it, huh?' By talking to your actor in this direct and immediate way, they will instantly respond as if they *were* the insulted employee: The emotion you were looking for will spontaneously arise, and if you do a take right after that, you can bet your 'employee' will show the boss that they won't be pushed around anymore. What you've done is, instead of asking directly for the result you want ('angry'), you've juiced them up with the FACTS that will make them angry, letting the actor put two and two together and coming up with the anger themselves. In this way you get the result you want, but the actor feels organically connected to the situation, and therefore the emotion is a lot more spontaneous and authentic."

WHY SAG (THE SCREEN ACTORS GUILD) IS NOT YOUR ENEMY

That one tiny acronym, SAG, seems to make filmmakers go wide-eyed and ultimately kinda stupid. They worry about the paperwork, the cost, and the possible issues with distribution, *and so they just don't deal with it.* And that, my friend, is stupid. Developing a good relationship with SAG when you're a first-time filmmaker can only create a win-win situation in the long run, especially once you're on to bigger projects.

Veteran producer Steak House explains it to us:

"SAG is very important for the low-budget movies; you don't have to pay for anything upfront, you're just agreeing to certain terms. Like if the film plays on television or gets distributed [where you are paid money for the rights to your film], the actors will get paid a certain minimum. When you do a short film there are expectations that it's only going to screen in film festivals. But by signing a SAG agreement, if it does make money, you're agreeing to pay the actors their rate. The rules are there for a reason. Take care of your actors, because you don't want them to feel neglected. You never know in ten years' time where the agents or managers of those actors are going to be. They could be heads of distribution companies or production companies, and they're going to need to say, 'Yeah, I remember her, she was good. She knows what she's doing.' It should just be part of the process, so just deal with it like a professional."

And when dealing with your actors it's imperative that they feel that you not only know what you're doing but that you also want to protect them. If an actor comes on board for free and you turn around and make a profit on your film for thousands of dollars (not likely, but it could happen), then you want to return to those actors and pay them a fair rate.

CARE AND HANDLING OF YOUR ACTORS

Be very careful about what you say to actors in the casting session *and* on-set. Even in a big city like Los Angeles (where there are literally tens of thousands of people vying for acting work), many actors know one another through classes or work and they talk about the directors they're working with. If you develop a not-so-great reputation within the indie actor scene, word will spread quickly—*very* quickly. Be respectful, be on time, and know exactly what you want from your actors. Like I said early on, your girlfriend is not an actress. Okay, maybe she is, but she probably isn't a good one . . . yet. You'll know, in your gut, if she's up to the performance. And if she's not, do not, and I mean it, DO NOT ignore your instincts. If I had a nickel for every film I've seen that had a great script, good camera, and good tone that was excruciating to get through because the lead was unwatchable, I'd have enough money to *pay* Halle Berry her quote to act in my next short.

And the opposite is also true. A standout performance can change a cliché script into a watchable and *programmable* film. Think about that in casting and on set. Stand and deliver for your script because when people are tired, and have been subjected to forty-seven camera moves, in the end it will only be you who can encourage them to endure in order to get the shots you need.

How a director treats her actors is paramount to the success of their film. Aurora Guerrero is part of Los Angeles–based Womyn Image Makers (WIM). WIM is comprised of four Xicana independent filmmakers and artists, Maritza Alvarez, Dalila Mendez, Claudia Mercado, and Ms. Guerrero. Since 1999, they have created shorts such as *Pura Lengua* (2005 Sundance Film Festival), *Viernes Girl* (HBO/NYILFF), and most recently *Aquí Estamos y No Nos Vamos* (2006 Los Angeles Latino International Film Festival). Because her films always have this depth of character, I approached Aurora to provide some insight on how she works with actors, and she shared this valuable piece of information:

> "When I work with actors, I concentrate on creating a nurturing space for the actor to be able to connect their personal lives to the characters they will be embodying. The key to creating that safe space is building trust with your actor. The way I build trust is by sharing my own personal stories that open up a two-way relationship between myself and the actor. We become vulnerable with each other, which oftentimes makes the actor feel like they aren't alone in that process. Once that trust is there, not only does the actor find personal experiences to use as a bridge to the character and story but the actor is also open to taking risks with you as

you go into production. That has been extremely helpful to me as a director."

Man, directing actors for first-time directors can be unnerving. When you wrote the script and envisioned the end result you already set into motion a particular visual. You've already imagined how the actors would deliver their lines, how they'd move their bodies, what exit and entrance strategies they'd take, but real-life shooting can be a very different experience. Be patient with yourself but also know as much as possible before you get on set. While making movies, disaster is always looming—be a step ahead of the game as much as possible. Alison Kelly drives the point home:

"Usually, if I'm feeling a director is not up to the task, then the actors are feeling that too. Because I operate* the camera on 90% of a shoot I end up having a connection to the actors insofar as I'm lighting them and I'm the closest person to them, and they look at me a lot when they're done with the take. I'm their immediate audience. It's up to me to maintain their level of trust and intimacy. Even if they're not aware of the camera operator being there, you can see when they're getting frustrated. I'm really, really aware of the mood of the actors on set. There have been productions that I've worked on where there's a vacuum at the top; people feel like there's nobody running the show. If I'm feeling that, then so are a lot of other people. I think then, the best thing you can do as a DP in that situation, is to be as supportive as you can for the director. And to never, ever turn and lose confidence. Because the second that you turn, it changes the whole mood on set. And it's not just the actors who

---

* Many DPs hire a Camera Operator whom they tell where to move the camera. Alison is noting that she doesn't often do this.

begin to jump ship, it's the whole crew. I've seen it happen and as soon as the grips and electrics lose confidence in what's happening with the director, it's such an uphill battle to get anything done. Generally people who work on shorts are underpaid or not paid at all, and they don't want to be there if they feel like they're wasting their time. Nobody wants to be a part of something that's just going to be a stupid movie."

Adrienne Weiss's student Katie Wallack says:

"I always check in with the other actors I'm working with. Sure I'll go to the director first, but if they're not coming up with the answer I need then I'll go to my peers and see if they've got some clarity. Make sure we're all on the same page. As well, most directors have everything in their head and sometimes are unable to express this to me, the actor, in a way I can bring to life. So often I'll ask the director not what I want [actor's motivation] but what am I *doing* in this scene? You know, what's my action versus what am I feeling. I mean, you don't just get up there in front of the camera and *feel*. What you're doing can often inform performance. A new director can even say 'I'm not sure' because then I have hope we can work it out together; they can even say 'What do you think?' because I don't expect directors to know *every-thing* about this character going into it, I really like working it out together. But when they start overexplaining or giving vague direction I stop listening and start losing confidence, which is always a bad sign."

Treat your actors as well as you can afford to. Always make sure there is at least one PA assigned to the actors (more than one if you have the resources), always make sure to have appropriate craft service and meals available to them. And if you can't have great food for them on-set, then let them know that up front! That way they can prepare for themselves, taking care of their bodies and minds so they can give you the best they've got to offer.

And if you want to have them come back the next day of shooting, know what you want from them, be on time, and don't waste their time on-set with crew squabbles, lack of preparation, or lengthy lighting setups without the benefit of stand-ins (people who are of the approximate height, weight, and skin tone of the actor who will be lit).

Kelli Garner (*Thumbsucker, The Youth in Us, Dreamland, Lars and the Real Girl*) shared what a really great director can do:

"I remember the detail that Josh [Leonard, dir. *The Youth in Us*] had laid out. I had a hard scene to do, to die gracefully and believably. I remember Josh and everybody around had helped set this room up with balloons and pictures of, 'I miss you and I love you.' There was even this one cube where Josh had put these pictures of this little blond girl all around it. Those were the little things that popped my emotion. As an actor, I've learned that I never want to act from the head, and the deeper I can get in my body physically, will draw all these emotions that are connected to it. And these small, beautiful little details that the whole crew pulled together surprised me. It's what makes a special scene in a short or a feature, when everybody gives you everything they have. And Josh was so detail-oriented that I didn't have to do anything. What sucks about films is not knowing what type of director you're going to be surrounded by. But if I sit here and think about it, there's not a big difference between a short and a feature, it's all just what makes a great director and what they allow in the moment. It's a lot harder to work on a short and what makes a great short film is when you watch a story unfold in eleven minutes, and you're like, 'I know those characters so well.'"

WHY WOULD SHE WANT TO WORK WITH ME??

There wasn't a single actor I spoke with who avoided first-time directors—and that is some great news for us all. Jane Lynch (*Best in Show, The 40-Year-Old Virgin, For Your Consideration, Talladega Nights, The L Word, Friends, 7th Heaven*, and so many more) is one of those actors we all dream about casting:

> "I love working with first-time directors! I tend to feel maternal towards them like, 'How can I help *you*?' and to be honest it helps me take the focus off of myself! ('How do I look in this? How am I coming across in this scene?') I just love encouraging new people, I try to be as nice as possible, and it's such a great thing to watch somebody coming into their own. First-time directors can sometimes have a really strong idea of what the scene is about, but often they are so busy and overwhelmed with what's going on that they're actually really happy that you [a seasoned actor] already bring so much to the table making *you* one less thing to worry about. I've worked with first-time directors who are so willing to let you do your own thing. So happy and so grateful that you're there actually teaching *them* something. They know that you are going to give them exactly what they've dreamed about all along and that not only takes the pressure off them but it gives me as an actor a lot of confidence. It must just be a *relief* for a first-time director who's got so much on their plate already to not have to also worry about the performance of a seasoned actor, and that is something every first-time filmmaker should have at least one of on cast—somebody who has done this many times before."

And, finally, do not treat your actors like they're set props providing a backdrop to your stellar camera work, crane shots, several-thousand-dollar production design, and dreams of Sundance. Chase Gilbertson, another one of Adrienne Weiss's students, encapsulates one major mistake many first-time filmmakers make:

> "So many first-time directors, or younger directors are just going for what I call a 'circus' production. What *was* an interesting script becomes secondary to camera movements, abrupt cuts and complicated blocking. As an actor, I just get pissed off. Obviously if I'm doing your film the story was good enough in the first place but now instead of simply telling a good story you're trying to make a Hollywood blockbuster. Yeah you've got a lot of cool toys but ultimately what is the end result? What happened to the story?"

See? Everyone, including the actors, wants you simply to tell us a compelling story that is visually interesting. No toys required.

7

Production
(Or What Happens If Your
Location Is Adjacent to
a Crack Addict)

Okay, so you've thugged it out and written your script, you've had a bunch of people read it, you've perfected it, you've rounded up a producer and dollars, you've got your crew and your dream cast. Now what?

YOU MAKE A MOVIE! It's time to take a stroll through the process of production. Production can be either magical or diabolical. You get to decide which path your on-set experience will take. You need determination, high emotional intelligence, skills, and a bunch of people with *more* skills to succeed in production with all of your shots in the can. And that is a combination of your Genius-Surround and your Big Belief. And what else? Ah, yes, flexibility!

CREATING ON-SET MAGIC

Part of what good planning in pre-production does for you and your film is it sets you up for on-set magic! Deciding what scenes to shoot first can be crucial. That first day of shooting sets the tone for the rest of the shoot. You get to see how your crew works under pressure and they get to see how prepared you are. People are usually fresh and ready to do whatever it takes. That first day is your day to prove you've got the chops to make a great film. Carter Smith shares an experience on *Bugcrush*:

> "With locations and actor schedules, the first scene needed to be the scene in the smoking pit. And, really, we felt like *if* we accomplished that enormously emotional scene on that first day we would *know* that we were doing something amazing. The crew was amazing. I did a great job choosing people who truly believed in the project. I did a lot of prep with every department and with some crew members working on the film for at least two months before we actually shot it. It was worth every moment of prep."

With the films I've shot so far, the difference between *Dani and Alice* and *Happy Birthday* was enormous. One was a drama about domestic violence, the other a comedy about sex toys and pregnancy. The place that I pulled my strength from on both films was paramount to the success of their respective shoots. It doesn't matter if your narrative film is a drama, comedy, or something in between. Your attitude toward the content of your script and the preparation you do to accomplish the storytelling will, to a large degree, determine the success of your shoot.

LOCATIONS TO DIE FOR

Pick something *simple*. Usually the first thing you start looking at is locations. It is locations themselves (along with production design) that help to create the story you want to tell. There isn't a single filmmaker out there who doesn't have a "location story" to tell that usually starts really badly and ends with a gift from the heavens. Allow me to share a couple of my own from my experiences working on both *Dani and Alice* and *Happy Birthday*.

Cabrini Snyder is a Black entrepreneur in Los Angeles and one year she decided to open her own nightclub/restaurant. It was perfect for my shoot! I'd be supporting another Black businesswoman, we wouldn't have to worry about the content of the script, and it was perfectly located in the city. I approached her and she generously allowed us to shoot the bar scene of *Dani and Alice* there.

Now, her bar was beside a seemingly innocuous small business. The owner? An *allegedly* cracked-out *alleged* member of a white supremacy group.

As soon as the cameras started rolling he started drilling, hammering, and playing the radio at ear-splitting volume while intermittently screaming his blistering opinions about people of African descent through the walls. The surrounding business owners were lovely and apologetic. Fortunately, on this shoot I actually had a permit for that location, so he couldn't call the police on us. We, however, could call the police on him. But no matter what (yes, the LAPD showed up), he continued to create as much noise as possible the moment I called "Action."

Now, as I've already established, Effie T. Brown is a great producer. While I was smashing my sunglasses to smithereens in the alley beside the buildings (it *was* the first day of shooting—I was a little on edge, plus I got them for five bucks in Venice Beach), she was negotiating and strategizing.

After speaking directly with the *alleged* crack addict white supremacist, she realized that we'd have to work around him. She explained New York Calls to me: This is when you call CUT when you mean ACTION and you call ACTION when you mean CUT. I call CUT, he stops drilling and *allegedly* goes back to the pipe. I call ACTION, he drills and we talk about the next setup. It worked. Kevin Lau, my on-set assistant and filmmaker in his own right (*Year of the Dog*), loaned me his sunglasses, and we were back on track.

Let's take a moment here and remember what we've learned about surrounding yourself with people who know more than you do, are seriously adept at their job, and are always working toward a great and successful shoot—the Genius Surround. If I didn't have Effie, Roger, and Christo on that shoot I might very well have been writing this book from jail. I was so stressed, angry, and without the solution to this seemingly deal-breaking problem that things could have been very rocky without seasoned producers on board.

On *Happy Birthday* we were lucky to have awesome location owners *and* neighbors. We used one location for the living room, the bedroom, an exterior, and one of the bathroom scenes. On-set in the home of Rachel Friedman life was perfect. She was supportive, kind, and, most important, patient. (Remember when I mentioned the lack of preparation on that shoot? We were supposed to be there from 8 a.m. until 6 p.m. *at the latest*—we didn't even start packing up until well after midnight.)

Without her great home we would have been scrambling to find not one location but four. Again, we lucked out when one of my producers, Jon Johnson, found us a location that could triple as a bar, a restaurant, and another exterior. Another example of the genius surround. I cast Julie Goldman, and Rachel was her best friend. I hired Jon Johnson, who gladly came on board after working with me in New York City at the Starlight Lounge, and he came through with both financing and locations.

These are examples of locations gone very wrong and very right. On larger-budgeted shoots you may be able to hire a locations manager who would be in charge of dealing with both *alleged* crack addicts and pretty Jewish girls in Brooklyn. Many of you will not have that kind of budget so it may be a wise thing to give up this responsibility to one of your producers or other key crew. Save yourself. Save your sunglasses.

ON-SET ETIQUETTE

And, again, be nice about it. You do not want the setups to slow way down because you were a jerk to the gaffer or one of his colleagues. This isn't the army, it's a film set. People are working hard (often at below their normal feature film day rate if it's a short) to realize your vision. Be mindful of that truth. Steak House shares her wisdom:

> "Be generous. Be as generous with your crew as you want them to be with you. I am interested in the personality of the director before I say I'll read their script. Get your expectations in order. I've met a lot of directors that are delusional. They think they're the next P.T. Anderson, and you know what—maybe they are, but not yet. It's the difference between pride and arrogance. Pride—good; arrogance—bad. I've done this enough times to be able to say 100% that when the director shows up on set with a smile on their face, with an 'I'm the luckiest guy in the world, I get to make my movie!' attitude, the crew responds in spades. People get behind you, the actors feel it, the crew feels it, and all that great energy gets directed right back to you. I've heard this over and over again from crews who make their decision to work with you based on the personality of the director. Is the set going to be professional, fun, and respectful? If the answer is not so much they walk away regardless of the credit they might get or the money you're paying."

And I've heard the same thing about the producer's attitude toward the rest of the crew. You choose a producer based on her ability to get things done, but it cannot be at the cost of the integrity of the set, as Madeleine Olnek points out:

"Most importantly, the producer should be someone who is always on your side and presents a unified front with you (and the film), as opposed to someone who is just thinking about how they are coming across. Otherwise you may find yourself in a good cop/bad cop situation, where *you* are the bad cop, and the producer is saying things to the DP like 'Gee, I'd like to get you lenses [for the camera], but I talked to the director, and she said she wouldn't pay for that.' It is often very hard for artistic collaborators to understand when their request for something that is very important to them is turned down, and when the amount is discussed in a vacuum with no other sense of the costs for all the other departments, and that vacuum amount cannot be paid (and that is blamed on you). It makes them feel underappreciated, it creates resentment and it damages their ability to work well with you. In a case like this, a good producer would say something like 'Sorry, but there isn't any money in the budget for that,' so immediately the person gets a sense of the bigger picture and the situation is neutralized. A good producer always puts the movie rather than themselves first, and ironically that makes a better movie, which ultimately makes them look better in the long run."

I wholeheartedly agree. And this circle of positive energy includes your director of photography. On *Dani and Alice*, Geary McLeod kept his crew motivated not by being a hard-ass but by being conscientious and having a lot of fun. He made sure they ate before he did, that we had enough PAs to help them get their job done, he let them shut the set down after the allotted number of hours they'd signed on for had passed (while I cried in the corner lamenting not being able to make that *one last shot*), and he massaged my shoulders assuring me we'd get those shots the next day. And we did. Also, remember it's the DP who is essentially standing for ten hours a day (while you and the producer can sit and watch the monitor in video village). I was not only impressed by his attitude, I was inspired by it. Having Geary's million-dollar smile made everyone on the shoot feel respected and important, including the actors, which is critical.

Same thing happened on the shoot of *Happy Birthday*. The director of photography, Alexa Harris, never stopped joking and laughing with the actors, her crew, and the PAs. She even made sure to include the often-ignored hair and makeup department (Angela Marinis, who came all the way to New York from Los Angeles just to help out).

As I noted previously, this was such a low-budget shoot that was understaffed from the top down, having Alexa there laughing even when things were going wrong really made a huge difference. In the moment, of course, I wanted to kill her! What was there to laugh about? We were hours behind in the schedule! People we were counting on hadn't shown up! We'd lost a key location! But let me say for the record, retrospectively, she had the perfect attitude and personality to handle all these unforeseen challenges.

ON-SET ATTITUDE

Your attitude on-set is indicative of how the shoot will turn out. I've been on plenty of sets where the director was either hiding in video village (where the monitor and "director" chair is set up) forcing the producer to deal with the crew, or they were walking around set checking in on almost every crew member. While I don't think you want to be that director asking a million questions that are essentially none of your business (*Wow, how many C-stands did we rent?*), I do think it's important for the crew to get a sense of who you are. Hiding in video village isn't the way to make that happen.

I asked several producers how they dealt with directors who

were difficult to deal with (not you or me, of course, but *they're* out there). Allen Bain (*Julia, Camp, Cry Funny Happy, Manito, XX/XY*), producer and owner of The 7th Floor in New York City, shares his philosophy:

> "The arrogance of directors is such a hard topic. We joke around about it as part of our job being like babysitters or psychologists. As a producer you're dealing with lots of personalities. So we have directors that we have a great relationship with, but they're arrogant or difficult. So you just have to know how to navigate that and handle their crew. It doesn't mean the film's going to be worse. Sometimes it's actually better. You can't really change someone who's an arrogant person, but you have to know how to tweak it. Also, as producers we're sort of casting agents in being able to put together a team. So if you have a really arrogant director, you have to find a tough-as-nails crew to deal with that person. If you have a nice soft director who knows what they want but they're not going to drive people to death, then we need a crew who will complement that as well."

Production is your moment to truly shine. And I want to give you some practical advice for dealing with on-set issues, because it's nerve-wracking to be a first-time director. There are going to be many people asking questions that you may or may not have the answer to. So many things that can (and do) go wrong. But if you can take that nervous energy and turn it into excitement you will find yourself very happy with the end result. Filmmaker and sound recordist Erin Greenwell (*Big Dreams in Little Hope*, aka *Mom; Commitment Ceremony;* and *Overnight Book*) states:

> "Quite honestly, the biggest thing you can do as a director on set is say 'yes' or 'no' with vision. My best days were when I kept it simple with answering and stayed true to

the cause. My worst days were when I said 'What do you think?' or hid in a corner while the shoot blurred by. The intense pressure of leading can also be a glorious feeling when a cast and crew are happy and moving. If the opposite is occurring, chances are you floated away, wishing you were on a sandy beach sipping drinks or on a mountain yelling your lungs out—alone. Remember that what shows up on the monitor is separate than what's screaming inside your stressed-out head."

INSURANCE

You will not be able to pick up your equipment (camera, lights, etc.) from a rental house without a Certificate of Insurance that covers the theft, damage, or loss of said equipment. Never. Ever.

For my first film I had insurance through the *foxsearchlab*. Oh, and yes, I had three producers and a seasoned production manager on my team who dealt with details like this. On *Happy Birthday* I had to deal with it myself. And, yes, I forgot about insurance *entirely*. That is, until the day before we were to start shooting, when Daniel Farmer at HotCam NY (who were supplying the equipment) called and asked me to fax him a copy of my certificate of insurance. Uh, what kind of certificate?

I frantically searched my cell phone address book for a member of my genius surround and found DeMille Halliburton, who is a Vice President at DeWitt Stern of California, an insurance agency with offices in Los Angeles. I texted and e-mailed SOS messages to him. Since he's a true professional, within an hour I had all the information necessary to know which type of insurance I needed and at a price the production budget could bear. I was able to fill out the forms and pay online, and within minutes, Katherine Wong in DeMille's office faxed the certificate to Daniel, and Daniel helped load the equipment into our truck. DeMille breaks down the insurance scene for us:

"Many filmmakers might be used to using their own equipment so when they move on to a higher-end camera, or have to rent light packages, they forget that all the rental houses require insurance. You don't have to buy thousands of dollars of insurance for your short but you need to cover at least the equipment you'll be using. I'd say a thousand-dollar budget line would cover most short film needs. But if you're going to be shooting on location with SAG [Screen Actors Guild] actors, know that SAG requires a certain type of insurance that covers the actors should they get hurt; if you're going to be shooting with moving cars all of that equipment needs to be insured; if you're using guns or anything like that on-set you'll need special insurance for that. All of this stuff should be old news to your producer, whose name is usually on the Certificate, but as the director you want to make sure your set is insured. I remember working with a guy who was shooting on location in New York City. I convinced him he needed full liability insurance and Workers Compensation insurance. He was reluctant but in the end he spent the money. In a bizarre and absolutely horrible twist of fate, a production assistant was killed accidentally in a car accident on-set. They were covered."

PERMITS

Permit rules are different in every city. You will have to contact your local film commission and find out what those rules are. For example, in New York City, you can shoot without a permit as long as you are not mounting the camera on a tripod. In Los Angeles, the police don't care how you're shooting—they want to see a permit issued by the city. Period.

I think you should always get permits to shoot on location. It's the professional thing to do, it's the legally correct thing to do, and it saves you headaches when you're shooting on location—you have a legal document from the city approving your shoot. Producer Steak House comments:

> "If you don't have a permit just know you may get shut down [by the police], so have a back-up plan or be a great smooth talker. One time we were stealing shots outside a hospital and my lead actor dropped his prop gun when he got out of the car. Next thing you know I was talking to five cops. It took me a minute but I convinced them to let us finish and that the gun was fake, but it could have gone the other way. We had a permit for the previous eighteen days that we could show them and it was our last night. Every shoot day is a miracle on an indie and every now and then the miracle doesn't come through, so be ready with plan B."

Have I always used permits? Maybe. Do I know many film-makers who shoot without permits? Perhaps. But in the end, the drama that could ensue without them isn't worth it. Get permits.

BREAKFAST, LUNCH, DINNER, AND CRAFTY

My very first job in filmmaking was Craft Service, otherwise known as Crafty. This is the area where you have snacks and coffee for the cast and crew throughout the entire shoot. It was an ultra-low-budget feature shoot and since I'd never done it before, I had no idea what exactly I was supposed to be supplying other than coffee (which I only knew because along with the cube truck rental they gave me this 100-gallon coffee percolator). I quickly found out on the first day when my chips and dip didn't go over so well. I wrangled my second mom (yes, I'm pretty lucky to have two), J.S., to help me. She's a whiz at stuff like this. We went to the supermarket and stayed up all night making food. Day Two saw delicious sandwiches, omelets, chips and salsa, fruit, and Red Vines licorice. (Note: If you don't have Red Vines at Craft Service bad things might happen to you.)

Every producer I talked to said that one of the biggest budget lines on a short is food. And as the director you really want to feed your crew well. Though if you know you can only pay for one meal (usually lunch or dinner), be sure to have your 1st AD note on the call sheet that people should come to the set already having eaten. If the cast and crew know there will only be Craft Service until the dinner break they'll come prepared. And no, you don't have to have the catering be from an expensive restaurant, but fast food isn't your answer either. Take notes from my students at Inner-City Filmmakers, where many of them had their moms cook for the cast and crew—hot-off-the-grill pupusas can go a long way.

REMEMBER TO BREATHE

In the end, what really counts is that you made a movie. There are hundreds of people out there talking about making a movie—but you did it. Take a moment, sit back, and pat yourself on the back! Filmmaker Kami Chisholm (*Ftf: Female to Femme, The Insomniacs*) shares a shining moment in making her last short film:

"The most exciting part of production was our last day of shooting. We were about to get thrown out of our location, but we still had to do the most complicated shot of the shoot, which involved rigging the camera above the bed at a 90 degree angle. It was taking a long time to set up, and I was very nervous, as this was the opening shot of the film. When the camera was finally ready, I made a decision to put all the constraints of the situation out of my mind and to focus on *getting the shot*. I didn't want to rush and get only one take that didn't work, which can often happen in these situations. We did a number of takes and nailed it. In the end what I am most proud of is that I kept a cool head and stayed focused on the objective: getting what I needed to make the film work. And I surrounded myself with an awesome cast and crew who never gave up."

And while it sounds like a cliché, the most valuable advice I can give you is to have a good time. Seriously. It took a lot of work to get to this point and you will never again be able to feel this magical moment of being a first-time filmmaker. Enjoy it. Be prepared . . . and enjoy it.

8

Post
(Remember: Homicide Is Illegal)

Post-production is what happens after you shoot your film. From editing to music, to sound editing and mixing, this is the one area most up-and-coming filmmakers have little knowledge about. Ah, but you already knew that, so you have since heeded my advice in Chapter 5 and hired a Post-Production Supervisor . . . right? *Right?*

No? Okay my friend, let me further outline why you need to approach post-production as earnestly as you approached your film in pre-production.

In those early days of being a baby filmmaker on *Dani and Alice,* I took my Dolby tape (from my sound mix at Soundelux/Todd A-O) to Color by Deluxe film lab along with my opticals (those are the credits—I'll explain those later). Marc Fishman, my customer rep at Deluxe, called to say, "Hey, Roberta, you left your sound tape here." I was speechless. Wasn't it supposed to go with my film?? I immediately recovered—okay, I lied—and said, "Oh, wow, right, thanks, I'll be right over to pick it up." I then called a friend who explained what happens to your sound (when you shoot on film) once it's mixed.

Don't be me. Both do your homework *AND* hire a Post Supervisor.

Because post-production is the most overlooked part of the process for first-time filmmakers, you may want to kill everybody you encounter. And, yes indeed, they all may be not-so-secretly wanting to kill you too.

The neg cutter is speaking gibberish (to you), the optical house's quote is several hundred dollars more than originally budgeted, the sound guy thinks it would be cool to add screaming hyenas to the background of your love scene, and the composer wants music under *everything*.

And you are exhausted, broke, and your pals have stopped returning your calls *and* your text messages.

You're sitting either at Color by Deluxe with your dailies or with your editor watching footage on his computer. Or perhaps you're watching video playback on-set. All of your hard work and that of the cast and crew you roped into working with you is right before your very eyes.

I have yet to meet a filmmaker who upon seeing her footage for the first time, didn't want to simultaneously bust open a bottle of Champagne, and move to another country to take a job as a bike courier. This is normal.

Repeat it three times out loud: "This is NORMAL." There will be moments of footage where you love your actors, want to buy your DP a vacation home in Maui, and take out an ad in *Variety* on behalf of your producer. And a fraction of a second later there will be tears welling up in your eyes, your heart will start racing, and the saliva will dry up in your mouth as you see some of the worst shots, lighting, performances, and blocking of your life.

THIS IS NORMAL.

When you find yourself in the beginning of your post process, don't ask yourself, "What have I done?" Only, and I mean it, *only*, ask yourself, "What am I going to do with what I have?"

Edit the film you have—not the one you wish you had.

I asked everyone who I interviewed for this book about post

(because it tends to be when filmmakers suddenly develop drug and alcohol problems) and just the word "post" made their eyes widen and mouths go dry. Steak House happily notes:

> "What a filmmaker wants to avoid is finding themselves on their own once he or she wraps shooting—[it] really is *all about* creating a *team* of people from the beginning to help you get your script to its completion in post-production. Whether you call that person or people producers, co-producers, line producers, or post-production supervisors—get that team together! I'm like the super hands-on guy who can take a movie from producing or line producing straight through post, but not everyone is. One of my producing partners, Julie Vizza, is also a really great editor, so we're able to map out the entire film beginning to end before we even start shooting. Because she's an editor she knows all things post and she also understands story, which is everything in post, because you have to understand the pivotal points in the film to be able to edit around performance, low production values, or if, sadly, you weren't able to get all of your shots. I've learned a lot about story just working on shorts with her. My other partner, Dominic Ottersbach, has the very necessary skills required to diligently be dotting the i's and crossing the t's all the while I'm loudly juggling the rest of our production needs in the air. Look, as far as post goes, if you've never done this before, then you better hire someone who has."

What most filmmakers (who didn't go to film school—and some who did) don't know is this: ALL post departments outside of editing need to work with a locked picture before they can do their jobs. In terms of scheduling, you can certainly send your composer and sound designer your rough cut to give them an idea of what is coming, but from what I hear, it's all a ruse. No one wastes their time doing any significant work until you send them the final picture, because ten times out of ten you and your editor make changes significant enough to make their preliminary work useless.

THE EDIT

Editing is your first foray into post-production. Remember, your homework for this section is Walter Murch's book *In the Blink of an Eye*. Go out and buy this book today. It is less than 100 pages, filled with truly extraordinary insights into the editing process. He's a genius; his book is genius; learn from him.

Now, something to remember is that there isn't anyone who likes to hear the phrase, "Oh, we'll fix it in post," less than your editor (okay, maybe your sound person). Sure, there are some things that can indeed be remedied in post (like color correction in underlit scenes or masking a shot in order to match another one), but if you didn't shoot it in the first place it cannot be magically re-created in the edit bay.

Now, on *Dani and Alice*, Geary and I discussed the shot list and the story boards to such great length that we, in the end, had enough coverage to provide an editor with all the tools he would need to create a great story. What also helped was when scenes had to be cut because we ran out of time. I *already* knew, from breaking down the script so deeply, what I could get away with cutting and what I could not afford to lose.

Through Effie T. Brown, I was introduced to the incomparable Paul Heiman. Paul was a features editor who was doing Effie a low-budget favor by working with my short alongside another, *Un Día De La Vida* (written and directed by the fabulous Marco Orsini). I had worked on the rough cut with another editor for a few months, but we were unable to come up with a cut that was true to the vision of the story. And when Effie saw it she took me outside and said, "I'm going to find you another editor. *Today.*" To that editor's credit, he was working for free and admitted up front that he didn't really have enough "free" time to complete the film. I more than understood his position because working with first-time directors is not terribly easy on many levels, and editing is one of the toughest stages a film goes through. We're overconfident with some scenes and suicidal with others.

Paul was able to explain my story back to me in words I could understand and ultimately made me a better filmmaker. Paul explains, in his Louisiana drawl, what a good editor tries to do:

> "You're never really sure where things are going to fall in the edit, which I think makes filmmakers, especially first-time ones, *very* nervous. I always start the process with what I like to call my 'Rough Cut Speech.' Walking the filmmaker through that first assembly/rough cut edit always makes my job a whole lot easier. A good editor will explain in detail how this [their shots/coverage] is going to cut together. How to focus on brevity, pacing for emotional balance—I mean, are you making a lackluster featurette or a powerful short? A good editor can throw in some temp music so you can figure out your musical cues before you meet with your composer. And, I guess, finally a good editor is really there to help you be honest with yourself out of the eye of the producer on the film, or the actors you have to leave on the cutting room floor, or the crew that worked fourteen hours on a scene that just isn't working anymore."

Blessedly, after talking with Paul for five minutes I knew he was *the one*. And in two days he had what was the final version of the film. Did I get lucky? I don't think so. I just think, as when choosing your producer, choosing your editor is just as important. They should understand the story, care about the story, and like what they're looking at. And, of course, the right person *always* comes along when you're ready. Carter Smith knew he'd found the right editor on *Bugcrush*:

"Holle Singer had read the script from day one. We'd worked on commercials together and we clicked on the approach I wanted to explore with *Bugcrush*. I'd seen her work and Holle was as much a perfectionist as I was. She was amazing. I really think I found the editor that I want to work with for a long time to come. She knew what the pacing needed to be in order to be compatible. I'd leave for a week and let her work on her own and come back and the stuff she'd worked on was brilliant. One of the reasons the film is so long is because she kept me on point during the lengthy driving scene that I was stumbling over. Then it was brought to my attention that the Sundance deadline was September 30th. I was at home when I got [Roberta's] e-mail. It was one of those heart-dropping-to-the-pit-of-your-stomach e-mails. You were so purposely ambiguous. We e-mailed back and forth and when I finally realized that you liked the film I was very excited. Roberta Munroe likes my film. I'm going in the right direction. But everybody said to me, 'You cannot make a 37-minute film! No festival is going to take such a long short!' It was Holle who told me I could not cut it down. We went back and did ADR [Additional Dialogue Recording]* to accompany that scene. And it is *this* very scene that freaked people out the most. That took the film up several notches. You *knew* something bad was going to happen. Without that scene I don't think *Bugcrush* would have had the impact it did."

---

* ADR is when a director brings their actors back to record a voice over or re-record dialogue that wasn't properly recorded during the actual shoot. It's also referred to as "looping."

THE TECHNIQUE OF EDITING

When I was shooting *Dani and Alice* all I knew about editing was what I knew worked and what didn't, based on the time I spent programming films. Which means I knew how great editing could move a story along, but didn't necessarily understand the technical aspects of how one got there.

Not so with *Happy Birthday.* Because Paul and I worked in his home studio I spent many many many hours sitting (often lying) on his couch watching him create the magic. I would ask Paul, "Well, can't we just cut back to Julie [Goldman] saying blah blah blah?" He would look at me with compassion and explain, "Yeah, that would've been great, but you didn't shoot a single [only Julie in the frame] saying that."

Rats.

But then Paul, because he's a great editor, would continue with, "But what we can do is . . ." And this is the person you want to work with, the editor who is creative enough and has watched all of your footage, so that they are able to offer you alternate solutions to scenes that aren't working. But remember, if you didn't shoot it in the first place . . .

I knew after shooting *Happy Birthday* that my next project would be a feature. After Paul's compassionate divulgence, I told myself: *I will completely understand how editing works by the time this short is done.* Both Paul and Eric Escobar, if asked, would be able to recount with great clarity the many phone calls I made asking *questions* (one doesn't like to call them *stupid* questions . . . however, I'll let you make your own inferences here) about the intricacies of Final Cut Pro.

I did indeed learn a lot, not only about why shot lists and storyboards are important but why, as a filmmaker, your knowledge of how editing works is paramount to your success on-set. When the sun is going down, and you've only got 40 minutes to get a shot in, you'll know which one *really* matters to the edit.

You won't get caught up in the self-indulgent filmmaker moment (no judgment, we all have them) of forcing the crew to set up the "pretty" shot you've been waiting all day to shoot.

Instead, you will be the smart filmmaker getting the shot most important to telling the story and find plenty of time at festival Q & A's to be indulgent. Glenn T. Morgan, Supervising Sound Editor at Soundelux (Todd A-O, Ascent Media www.soundelux.com) has worked on such diverse projects as *Monster's Ball, Real Women Have Curves, The Mask of Zorro, Jackass: The Movie, Blow, Mission Impossible II, Home Alone, JFK, L.A. Story,* and *Open Water.* He shares what he's seen happen since the advent of computer editing software:

> "I remember when Avid first started to come into play, maybe in the late eighties, everyone kept saying the plus side is you'll be able to cut faster. You can cut faster, so you can cut more versions. So at the end of the day, have you finished your movie any faster? No. Have you been able to create more versions of your movie? Yes. The real problem is becoming a disciplined filmmaker. The argument is said that tape is cheap. But labor isn't. And when you're shooting all that footage, that's what you're wasting—labor."

MUSIC

Music can make the world of difference in helping to set the tone and pacing of your story. We all know the heavy piano and string music used in horror films to prompt you to be afraid—something bad is about to happen. And very few people in the film world don't know the theme from Darren Aronofsky's *Requiem for a Dream* (composed by Clint Mansell, performed by the Kronos Quartet and the string quartet arrangements were created by Pulitzer Prize–winning composer David Lang)—it was a masterpiece, a haunting masterpiece.

This is a wonderful example of how music leads you deeper into a story.

What we also know is that original music is the only way to score your short unless you've got plenty of money to pay for licensing fees. In order to understand music in film from a musician's perspective, I spoke with Paula Gallitano, who composed the music for both *Dani and Alice* and *Happy Birthday*. Paula is an award-winning composer/jazz pianist who has written and produced music for several artists from Lalah Hathaway to Cypress Hill. She has toured with the multi-platinum group *SNAP* as musical director and has composed music for many national ad campaigns, television shows, and film. She shares this:

"Scoring music for film to me is like creating a beautiful vision of perfection. Most times the process is one of intuition that translates into an imaginative and articulate musical experience. The delicate balance between the emotional landscape I create and the artistic intention of the director is most important. Oftentimes the director has been watching the film for weeks with temp [temporary] music or no music at all. For me the challenge as a composer is to be aware of the textures I create, the space, and many times the silence. To be imaginative and bold in my expression yet conscious of what the director has been listening to is key for me. Many times I find 'less is more' in executing a musical idea, and it can be exhilarating to defy convention and watch the scene play perfectly against new ideas. Sound design is yet another factor. Together, music and sound design create a soundscape that must work perfectly with one another. The sound design helps decide the instrumentation I choose to use. If it's possible to attend the studio mix of your film, it is always a lesson in learning many components to the process of a final mix. It is also the perfect opportunity to check out the depth and space of how your final mixes translate to the theater."

In experimental works music and sound design are often an essential aspect to the film's success. Experimental filmmaker Shirin Neshat talks about her process:

> "For me, the sound design has been one of the most important elements of my films since, as you explained, most often sound and music replace dialogue. Of course this has changed in my recent feature *Women Without Men*, where we do have dialogue, yet the sound design remains essential in conveying the emotional, rather spiritual aura of the narrative and the characters. In the past two films, I have had the honor to collaborate with Ryuichi Sakamoto, whose compositions are quite minimal yet highly emotional. His score went beyond conventional sound design; rather, it helped me conceptually to define various spaces (whether magic, real, or dreamlike), or the character (exploring personal and social dilemma). Ultimately, since my narratives tend to have a political overtone, particularly related to my country, Iran, the music tends to emphasize the universality and timeless dimensions of the subject matters."

SOUND—WITHOUT IT, YOU'VE GOT BUBKES

"Hold for plane."

The entire shoot comes to a screeching halt as the plane flies overhead just as: your documentary subject finally comes clean on why he molested his sister; your actor after four takes gets the line right; you're shooting in Prospect Park without a permit and the sun is going down, *fast*.

There isn't a filmmaker (or producer) I spoke to who didn't bring up the sound department as an area first-time filmmakers underestimate in importance. There is a common misconception that anyone can hold a boom (overhead microphone) and record sound. Just as your director of photography cannot be replaced by your earnest best friend, neither can the sound be recorded by the tallest person on set. Erin Greenwell, a filmmaker (*Big Dreams in Little Hope,* aka *Mom, Overnight Book, 21*), and a professional sound person, shares this:

> "Sound is one of the easiest elements to mess up on a set where everyone is in a rush (and therefore loud, impatient, and flustered—'We'll fix it in post!') and it's one of the most important ones to the success of your film! Therefore, you need a professional who can quickly strategize how to record the best sound, get out of the way, and protect the integrity of the surroundings. ADR is costly and it is nearly impossible to match performance later. Sound effects from a library often don't match the movie later either. A good sound recordist evaluates all the noises around them on set. Even the quietest room has layers of sound. In tandem is the rhythm; rhythm to the way people speak, camera choreography, and actors' movement. Picture editing and sound mixing are an extension of those noises and rhythms. If I can record all sounds separately on set, I can rebuild that world in the edit. Those elements (dialogue, Foley, general atmosphere) can distract from problems or reinforce themes in the story."

Additionally, I can tell you that amazing sound is indeed important when setting the tone for your film. And this can be done in post with a great sound editor. David Briggs, a highly recommended sound editor (he taught Erin Greenwell at CCNY), gives us some advice:

> "Short of collaborating with a sound-editing professional, the best thing a short filmmaker can do for their film is to start with a traditional dialogue edit; i.e., cleaning up and toning out their on-set production audio tracks. That in itself

is the first step toward creating a soundscape that invites the viewer in. In terms of additional sound design (ambiences, sound effects, music), I'm a huge fan of Foley effects, those little specific sound details [e.g., footsteps, doors closing, unwrapping a package] that can serve as an additional musical element to the film's 'score.' When properly selected, edited, and mixed, Foleys can support and punctuate characters' gestures and rhythms, adding focus, texture, and life to the world of the film."

UGH, HE SOUNDS LIKE HE'S ASLEEP!

Mixing sound once your film is done is one of those things that is actually kind of fun for you, the director (or at least it was for me). Here is where you can add layers of sound effects to enhance the story—and sometimes the performance. On *Dani and Alice*, Lisa Branch was a little nervous in one scene. We tried it several ways, but her voice kept going up octaves, which belied the words she was saying. In the sound mix, Glenn T. Morgan, Marc Fishman, Peter Staubli, and the awesome team from Soundelux were able to bring her voice down a few octaves, creating a believable moment. If I knew this was one of those things you can "fix in post," I wouldn't have taken so many takes!

Depending on your budget (or your ability to get favors for free or on the cheap), you might be in a home studio or, as I was on *Dani and Alice*, in a sound stage studio with more gadgets at your disposal than you could have ever dreamed of. Regardless of where you mix your sound, the sound editor you hire will be invaluable to your final product. When I talked with Glenn T. Morgan (Soundelux), he was clear about what you should be doing as a director:

"I've always believed that my role is the audio version of the set designer. I create the environment sonically as you will hear the story be told. A good sound job is a good sound job, and it shouldn't really be called sound *design*. And the [sound] mix is a blend of all the words and the music and the sound effects. There are times when the music will support you and get to the story, so you want to let each of those disciplines support the story and guide you through the journey. As hard as it may be to think about, you need to have a clear point of view. The most disconcerting thing about working for a first-time filmmaker is they're going to have anxiety. They're going to be insecure and that is sometimes masked by aggressiveness. But all can be forgiven if you're clear about what you want, and you're consistent. The most maddening thing is to not know, and keep changing your mind."

I mentioned earlier that giving your rough cut to your sound editor or composer can be a waste of time. But there are times when it isn't. Glenn offers some advice:

"What it comes down to is economics. It's applying your resources appropriately. There are guidelines. If you're doing a type of short that is sound-driven. If you're shooting a horror film, every time you hear that sound—something bad is going to happen. In order to make it compelling, you want to have some sort of template. There are some directors—if they're going to shoot a horror film they decide early on who their sound guy will be, and have some sounds prepared for them to play on set. It's not a common practice, but it does happen."

UH, YOU SPELLED MY NAME WRONG

Credits. Those are the carefully placed list of names of the people who worked hard to help you make your film. By this stage of the game you are usually exhausted, broke, and thrilled it's almost over. Be diligent, my friend. Make sure your producer or production coordinator kept a complete list of your cast and crew so you do not forget anyone at this stage. Believe me when I tell you that *you will not* remember the name of the person who came in to do craft service the day your mom had Pilates class. Also make sure you have the correct spelling. As someone whose last name can be spelled five different ways can attest, correct spelling *is* important.

Also, be mindful of how long your credit crawl is. Seems like it wouldn't matter, but I can tell you I've watched a ton of shorts that had a solid 12-minute picture running time that got bumped up to a total of 14 minutes with extensive, slow-moving credits. This final runtime, with credits, is what programmers are using to determine if your film fits into a program. No one is using the picture runtime. Yes, you must thank all the people who helped on the film, but you do have control over how long that credit crawl takes to roll. Be judicious. It is a common joke in programming meetings—*the credits took longer to watch than the film itself.* If I could change anything about *Dani and Alice* it would be to cut that ridiculously long credit crawl to half the two minutes it is!

HMM, WHAT'S THE WORST THING THAT CAN HAPPEN IN POST?

What many people don't know is that I actually shot a film in Toronto before *Dani and Alice*. It was called *Can I Get You Anything Else*. I brought on some great actor friends (I cast my father and my stepmother, Wilma, in lead roles—luckily, they were naturals), had a wonderful cinematographer, and a hard-working crew (mostly my best friends David, Michael, Denise, and Bob). We shot fourteen pages in twenty hours (!!!) on Thanksgiving Day at my friend Elena Embrioni's restaurant.

Shortly after the shoot wrapped I moved to New York City *and that was the last time I saw my footage.*

Lost. Gone. All the tapes in one box. Disappeared. Was I devastated? Yep. Did I look *everywhere,* even where it would have been impossible for those tapes to be (like under my ex-girlfriend's bed)? Yep.

I tell you this cautionary tale for one reason and one reason only. You, the director, are responsible for your film. At every stage. Buy TWO hard drives—one for the editor and one as a backup. Yes, it's a few hundred dollars added to your budget, but would you rather be out $300 or have your entire film go up in flames in your editor's garage fire? Always *know exactly* where your footage is—put that backup hard drive under your pillow, and, no, I don't care how uncomfortable it is to sleep on.

9

Distribution

The MPAA reports that about 2% of all feature-length films that get made actually secure a theatrical or DVD release in the U.S. And from what I understand, once you take out all the Sundance films that have stars in them, that number drops to about 1/2%. Yikes. In our digital age, the fact remains that the technology to make films has completely outrun the capacity to release them. As Tom Quinn notes in the foreword, distribution in the short film world can be quite difficult.

So while filmmakers across the globe are definitely celebrating the explosion of Internet marketing, user-generated sites (e.g., Revver), and self-distribution, the *first* thing you need to ascertain is if your film has any limiting elements that might prevent distribution. There is a list of Do's and Don'ts which are outlined in *Orly's Distribution Questionnaire* (this appears later in the chapter). The second thing you should know is that while distribution for short films isn't easy, it's certainly not impossible, but you have to have a solid plan *before* you make your film as to where you want to distribute it. This might inform your storyline content, locations, and talent (e.g., if you want to sell it to iTunes you probably don't want to have the word f*ck in every other line of dialogue, or full frontal nudity).

In order to cover as much ground as possible I've interviewed some veteran executives and self-distributing filmmakers. Because I firmly believe that you can indeed make *some* money back, here are a few ways to do that.

First up is Orly Ravid. Orly is the Vice President of Acquisitions and Distribution at Senator Entertainment's USA division. Formerly the Senior Vice President of Acquisitions and Senior Representative for Foreign Sales, Business Affairs, Theatrical, New Media, and Film Festival Distribution at Wolfe Video, it was Orly who brokered my deal for *Dani and Alice* at Wolfe. She and her business partner, Jeffrey Winter, are mavericks in niche marketing through their company, New American Vision (www .newamericanvision.com). I asked Orly when she thought filmmakers should begin thinking about their film's distribution. She replied:

> "*Before* they make their film. When one is making a film, a) one should start to have a sense for who the audience of the film is, and b) do what's necessary to make sure that film is distributable, to conceive of its appeal in advance so one can start setting up marketing for the film. And marketing starts with the packaging that you send to the film festival (or agent, etc.). Even though production is always harried and one always feels they don't have enough money, it really is short-term thinking to not spend that little extra time and money to take care of the artwork representation of the film, whether that's having illustration or photography that's really compelling. If you pursue publicity, you're not going to have any images to publicize the film if you don't do that. At the end of the day, almost no one is spending time trying to find you, or think several steps ahead about how good your short really is and who and how many will want to see it;

you have to do the thinking for people, for everyone. Also, if distribution is the goal, you need to not have music that's unclearable or anything else, like maybe not have a McDonald's restaurant in the background of a critical scene you cannot cut out."

I realize this may feel calculating for an artist. It's not. It's simply a different take on what we discussed in Chapters 1 and 2. Research your story, tell a story that matters to you, and do your homework. If you want anyone other than your mom to see your film, then step back from your script and truly envision who your audience is. And remember, as I mentioned earlier when writing your script, that sure it might be a cool nod to George Lucas to include a *Star Wars* poster in the background, but not so cool if no distributor can buy your movie because it's in every other frame.

SELF-DISTRIBUTION IS FUN . . . SORT OF

Of course one of the easiest ways to distribute your film is on the film festival circuit. Though this is the least profitable, as most films do not make money on screening at festivals (save for niche films like those with lesbian, gay, bisexual, transgendered content where screening fees are the norm—but still, you're not going to make twenty grand), they really are all about introducing yourself and your work to the world. As I explained earlier, you will probably not make your money back from a short film unless you were *extremely* limited in your budget. However, the benefit of getting a lot of play on the festival circuit is that it increases your visibility as a filmmaker (more on this in the film festival chapter). You can then turn this visibility into wealth-making opportunities down the road.

Filmmaker and Internet trailblazer Tiffany Shlain (www .tiffanyshlain.com) has self-distributed one of the top-selling short films on iTunes, *The Tribe*. She echoes Orly's advice as well as outlines what she did for her award-winning film, *The Tribe*:

> "Most filmmakers spend all their money, all their energy on the film. And by the time they're done, they're exhausted, they're broke, and they're depleted of energy. With all the tools available today, filmmakers need to recalibrate how they look at it. Finishing the film is just step one. Step two is just as crucial, and takes just as much creativity, takes just as much money: They need to outreach. What I did with *The Tribe* is I raised funding for *both* processes. I raised funding for making the film, as well as money for outreach. So as we were cutting the film we also made a discussion kit, we made our DVDs, we created a *robust* Web site, we planned a premier— regardless of whether we got into a top-tier festival like Sundance or not—to kick off the film. Anything that wasn't in our control, like getting into a big film festival, we didn't count on when planning distribution and marketing."

Leah Meyerhoff (www.leahmeyerhoff.com) shares how she entered the film festival circuit with *Twitch*:

> "I sent a rough cut into Sundance, which was probably a mistake. Then I sent less of a rough cut into Slamdance. It got in, and I flew out to Slamdance and had a great time. *Twitch* won one of the grand jury awards. That was a good starting point, because from there, I started getting tons of e-mails from other festivals requesting the short. And I started realizing that it's worthwhile to send your film out there. I made DVDs and postcards, and made a huge database of all the film festivals that looked good. I have this Word document that's like 100 pages long of festival contacts in chronological order. So I sent all these e-mails, and some of them said 'Yes, we'll waive the [submission] fee,' and

those are the ones I ended up submitting my film into. My film has played at 200 film festivals, and it was all through that early work I did. I started going to the festivals that would pay for me to come there."

TELEVISION & DVD DISTRIBUTION

If your film gets picked up by a distributor or garners enough prestige on the fest circuit, you can make *some* money licensing it around the world. Distributors of short films license for broadcast and digital (downloadable or online streaming) distribution deals worldwide. Sometimes they'll even license for DVD (home entertainment) compilations, which are usually limited to niche markets (such as gay and lesbian, or African American, or Sundance Shorts, or Academy Award shorts collection) or thematically selected shorts. Leah Meyerhoff notes:

"I had an offer from IFC [Independent Film Channel] right off the bat from being on the show but it was only for $500, so I said no. Instead I did the festival route, though at the end of the day, I ended up giving it to them anyway, but *not* exclusively. And then Realport, which is European television, bought it for a couple thousand dollars, and then Scandinavia TV also bought it. The music videos I sold [*Team Queen* and *Eternal Flame*] to Logo and MTV Europe. So television is where I feel short filmmakers can make the most money. While you're submitting to all the festivals you can, I feel you should try as many distribution platforms as possible, as long as it's *not* exclusive. I also started doing all kinds of DVD compilations but I have yet to make much money from any of these. And then there's the Internet. I think short filmmakers are able to find more of a home on the Internet now than ever before."

DVD short film compilations are not the most profitable things on the planet, but they can augment a filmmaker's profile, and make you a few thousand bucks. And of course, every now and again there is a short that, due to media attention, demands to be released as a stand-alone film, such as *Blair Princess Project* directed by and starring Paula Goldberg (which, incidentally, was released by Orly Ravid while she was still at Picture This). *Blair Princess Project* was released in 1999 on VHS and sold over 10,000 units.

YOUR SHORT AS YOUR PILOT

With the incredible leaps that network and cable television have made in the downloadable content arena, it is more important than ever to step outside of the feature filmmaking box. You may be surprised to see that the short film you have *already* made *is* your television pilot. Think about it—if you walk into a pitch meeting with the pilot already done, the executives can not only see your talent, they also have the blueprint for the show you want to make. This would be especially helpful to your career, since networks are less and less able to finance pilots and are sussing out shorts in lieu of taking a risk on your talents by forking out thousands of dollars. Expand your definition of what distribution is, because if you can get your short made into a profitable series, that *is* distribution!

There is definitely a difference between shooting a scene from your feature script and shooting a longer short that you hope to sell as a television series. A great example of this is the short film *The Ten Rules*, written by Michelle Paradise (www.michellepara dise.com) and directed by Lee Friedlander. It was "too long" by most standards (over 20 minutes); however, it was a solid story that created solid characters one could envision seeing on television week after week, and had audiences laughing worldwide. It took them a few years, but Paradise and Friedlander never gave up on it, eventually selling it to MTV Network's Logo, where it premiered in 2008 with the new title, *Exes & Ohs*. Michelle reveals her process:

"At the time, I didn't think of *The Ten Rules* as having the potential to be a television pilot simply because when I wrote and shot it—and this is only back in 2000 and 2001—there was nothing out there in the world to suggest that a lesbian television show was even possible, let alone desirable. *Logo* and *here! tv* didn't exist; *The L Word* didn't exist. Looking back at it now, though, I can absolutely see why the short got Logo's attention as a possible series. It wasn't a pitch they had to try and envision or a script they had to read, it was a finished product that they could actually watch. They could see the story, the point of view, the characters, and whether or not all of those elements had the potential to expand into six episodes, or eight, or eighty. That's one of the keys, I'd say, if your goal is to do a short that could be a pilot: Make sure all the elements of your project have that potential to expand. If your story isn't about something universal, at its core; if there isn't a clear point of view; if the characters lack the depth to take them through possibly as many as eighty episodes, then it won't work as a series. Keep in mind, too, that this is not an easy journey—nor is it a fast one. So no matter what happens, no matter how long it takes, just keep working. And never, ever wait for someone else to give you permission to be creative. *Exes & Ohs* wouldn't exist if I hadn't sat down in front of my computer in San Francisco and dared to stare at a blank screen and just start typing. That typing became *The Ten Rules* and *The Ten Rules* became *Exes & Ohs*. I am now the executive producer, writer, and one of the stars of my own television series. I am proof that it can happen. So don't wait. Don't make excuses. Just do it."

Lee Friedlander, producer, executive producer, and filmmaker (*The Ten Rules, Girl Play, Out at the Wedding, Exes & Ohs*), adds:

"When Michelle Paradise showed me her short script, we decided to raise the money and make it ourselves on a shoe-string budget. I believe it was a 32-page short, and at the time everyone told us to shorten it, that film festivals only wanted 15 minutes or under—I believe [Roberta] was one of those people [laughs]. But I really wanted to shoot it like a half-hour single-camera comedy so I could have some work to show in that arena for television jobs. It was important to me that it looked as good, sounded as good, and was the same quality as a mainstream show. We shot on a Panavision HD 24p, pulled in every favor, and spent a lot of time in post getting the pacing, style, music, and effects right. I went on to direct *Girl Play* and when MTV launched Logo I brought it to them to try to sell it for distribution. Initially, I met with Eileen Opatat and John Sechrist and *The Ten Rules* was on the reel that I gave them—and they loved it! We all started to develop the show, Logo grew, and Dave Mace and Pam Post came on board. We spent a couple years molding, growing, adding veteran writer and producer Billy Grundfest (*We the Jury, Mad About You, Academy Awards Show*) to the mix and as they say—the rest is history. A script, a pilot, a first-season order, and now Season 2 on its way! I truly believe that if we did not have this as a finished 'Pilot Presentation' the show would not have sold. If you are not a Greer Shepherd or David Kelley, networks have no idea if you can deliver. I don't think they would have let me direct the first episode of the series if I had not shown, through directing the short, that I could do it."

Because they showed the network that they could write and direct and act (Michelle Paradise is the lead actor in both the short and the show), Logo didn't need to go on blind faith. Dave Mace, Vice President, Head of Original Programming, notes:

"Since Logo is a very new cable network and because we don't have the same budgets of broadcast and other cable networks, we often rely on short films to serve as our pilot or 'mini-pilot' for the series. By eliminating the pilot step in the development process, we put all of that money back into the series and up on the screen—where it belongs. What short filmmakers who aspire to work in television need to know is they should be thinking in terms of television BEFORE they create the short film and not AFTER. Not all short films translate to a television series, especially if they weren't conceived as such. We look for concept, storylines, and character arcs that will have longevity. In other words, the short film has to set up a series that will last for five, six, or seven seasons in succession."

YOUR WEB SITE *IS* YOUR DISTRIBUTOR

As Tiffany Shlain has drilled into my head over and over these past few years, you've got to create a robust and engaging (meaning make people want to purchase your film off the site) Web site! You can sell your film online without a distributor. You might not get rich, but you might make a few dollars and create some excellent marketing for yourself. I spoke to Marc Rosenberg, who created one of the top filmmaker marketing Web sites in the U.S. (www.internetmarketingforfilmmakers.com) that for a very small fee walks a filmmaker through Internet self-distribution. Marc notes:

"I think if you latch two or three short films together and find a marketing hook, that can be marketable as a DVD. . . . I would say rather than trying to sell a single short for less money, you're better served teaming up with two other film-makers, forming a little company together, and marketing it together. And there's nothing wrong with a mixed bag if you have easy access to wide distribution. If you're doing your self-distribution this way, you're much better off targeting a niche audience and going after them hard. So a big part of the success of my film, *Zen Noir*, is the fact that we knew our audience. And I knew how to go find them on the Internet. That's one of the primary powers of the Internet, is you can go there to find niche audiences in large numbers. If you have a gay film, go find two more gay filmmakers and so on. I think it all depends on the individual group of filmmakers and how they want to promote it. There's nothing wrong with a collection of three gay comedies or three Asian com-edies, or three Asian tragedies. But you probably don't want to say that. You want to say, 'three powerful movies on the Asian experience.'"

Marc continues with the point that you shouldn't neglect the festival circuit, and that you needn't hold out for only the top-tier fests—start submitting to that larger pool.

"What's scary is that there's this message coming through the industry that is saying, 'Don't even waste your time with smaller film festivals.' I argue vehemently against that be-cause I had people look at my film and say, 'You're taking a horrible chance for leaving distribution for yourself. No-body's going to buy it,' and then a year later, it won seven or eight awards from small festivals, and then they say, 'Seven or eight awards from small festivals is not equal to Sun-dance,' but to the buying public, *it has value.* You can create a pedigree to your film. I didn't self-distribute because I think self-distribution is what everyone should do—I self-distributed because I had the capacity to do so, and I think it's important that everyone has the capacity to do so, in case they fall into the situation where they truly believe they have a distributable product and nobody else wants to market it, they can do it themselves. But I'll be completely up front about this: It's all about budget. If you make a movie for ten million dollars you *need* to get a distributor."

THEATRICAL RELEASE . . . IT COULD HAPPEN

The ultimate distribution dream is that every now and again a short can get programmed to be at the head of a feature, especially at an art-house theater such as one of the Landmark Theatres screens. Distributors do this occasionally on DVDs as well, but it's rare, and up until now one needed to have a 35mm print. This is changing quickly. In fact, so much is changing so fast in the distribution world that even seasoned distributors are facing constantly changing criteria. Tom Quinn of Magnolia Pictures (www.magpictures.com) talks about mounting the theatrical release of the Oscar-nominated narrative and animated shorts:

> "The expectation was that we would go out and try to build this program [Academy Award Short Film nominees] from scratch, and not be able to model what these films were worth, having no comparable films or platforms. That was the fun thing; we made it up as we went along. These films have really gone out with what I qualify as a very barebones budget and yet they appeal to a very upscale art marketplace. It takes an enormous amount of work to pull this off well, so you're going to have to learn really, really quick, and be incredibly creative, resourceful. You're not only working with a first-time filmmaker from halfway around the world; you're working with Disney, Pixar, Fox, Sundance Channel, Focus. I've seen every hurdle along the way. It's a pretty amazing miracle that we've been able to secure every

[Academy] short film nominee for the program. Every year, I don't know what's going to happen. It's not making anyone rich, but this year [2008], these films went out and grossed over a half million dollars. So that puts them in a really small group. They're performing at the top of their engagement."

RIDING THE INTERNET WAVE

Let's talk YouTube. Just when I'm thinking I'm a little old for YouTube, an awesome short film link gets forwarded to me and I'm hooked back in. There is something about YouTube that makes me excited about what I might find there. Adrenaline is pumping, I'm signed in, I'm searching for my friends' names or for more films from the director who got forwarded to me and blammo! an hour and a half has gone by.

And for me, that's what makes YouTube fun. You're like your own little studio mogul sitting in your living room finding some of the best (and definitely some of the worst) new talent the world has to offer. And, of course, every few months some renegade digital goddess uploads *Dani and Alice* and I must admit it is kinda cool to see that over *ten thousand* people have watched my movie! (Before Wolfe Video's legal department shuts them down.)

Now, like you, I always thought "How do you make money on YouTube when it's free to watch your film?" So I reached out to Sara Pollack, Film Manager for YouTube, and she helped clarify why putting your film online for free can actually, in the long run, make you money:

"Primarily, one of the biggest problems for films, even theatrically, is finding an audience. Audiences tend to take less risk in terms of what they're willing to spend money on. If you have this incredibly broad accessibility and there isn't a price tag involved, audiences are much more willing to take risks. So is putting your content up for free good for every single filmmaker? No. I don't think there are benefits for every kind of film. But if you're a lesser known filmmaker and you're trying to get exposure, and you're trying to introduce audiences to your work, I think you're going to have a much easier time doing that without a $14.99 DVD sale price tag. I would want filmmakers to be part of our program so they're generating service. It's about holding an audience and finding ways to monetize that audience once you have it. When we featured an independent feature on YouTube, it showed up on the iTunes top ten. This is all very new, so I can't point to thousands of examples, but we've seen that happen: People put up their content—and maybe it's because the quality is lower on YouTube and people want to see it on DVD—but interest is piqued and it can pay off. There are over one million unique views every day on YouTube—filmmakers can and do find audiences."

Over one million views? You would be crazy not to try to get a piece of that pie, especially if you've already done the festival circuit and haven't yet been picked up by a distributor. Sara explains further:

"Whether it's directly influencing DVD sales or digital downloads/views, or if it's just about sponsorship, or building an audience so the next time you create content you know you're going to be able to sell DVDs, or you're showing more traditional Hollywood companies that you have this audience online. Filmmakers are making very meaningful connections with their audiences, beyond the monetization. 1,000 views is like selling out a theater *twice*. So for filmmakers to make a film that has 100,000 people see it and have 4,000 people make comments or ask questions or post video responses, that's very meaningful, especially for a young filmmaker who's just starting to figure out who they are as a filmmaker."

And as if that wasn't already enough, they have now introduced The YouTube Screening Room, where you the filmmaker can submit your film to be considered as part of the Screening Room. I ran into Sara at the YouTube Lounge at the Los Angeles Film Festival 2008. Sara invites filmmakers to submit:

"We introduced The YouTube Screening Room to improve distribution opportunities for filmmakers beyond the film festival circuit. In addition to reaching a potential audience of hundreds of millions of people around the world, filmmakers can also share advertising revenue through the program. We hope all filmmakers will use YouTube as a platform for their work, and we look forward to featuring some of the most compelling, entertaining, and original content in The YouTube Screening Room. Filmmakers interested in being a part of The YouTube Screening Room can send an e-mail about their film to ytscreeningroom@youtube.com."

There are a number of user-generated sites other than You-Tube that offer filmmakers a global audience and some, like Revver (www.revver.com), also offer revenue-sharing opportunities. What this means for short (and feature) filmmakers is spectacular. For example, when YouTube featured Nash Edgerton's short *Spider* it became the fifth bestselling short on iTunes; four short films at the 2008 SXSW film festival were previously featured on YouTube; IFC picked up the broadcast and DVD rights to the feature film *Four Eyed Monsters* after it was featured on YouTube, and then, of course, there is the fact that with user- and filmmaker-generated momentum videos can be viewed millions of times. One of the most viewed videos on YouTube is a

10-minute narrative short, *Lo Que Tu Quieras Oir* [What You Want to Hear]. It was viewed over 70 million times. People! *Seventy million* views—I doubt there is a distributor out there who could promise you that.

What you will also find on YouTube and other sites like it is variety. I think we've sort of hit a wall in terms of what is considered great filmmaking, particularly in North America. And user-generated sites bring us back to the more grassroots aspects of filmmaking. Filmmaker Duncan Roy (*AKA, Method, The Picture of Dorian Gray*) shares this:

> "Popularity on YouTube is not being determined by anything other than word of mouth. I think that's where everything's going to change. In Hollywood everyone's after the next new young thing, and I think there are a lot of older people making extraordinary things, so the Internet will give more of a range. People are worried about the quality [on YouTube], but the cream always rises. The great thing about it is it's meritocratic. We are used to grainy images of ourselves or other people, like on surveillance cameras; those images are just as important as glossy images. We've got a range of images we can put together now, and I don't think any of those images are more important than another. It is similar to the forensic approach in the way I work: There's something going on in this room and we need to put together the evidence of what's going to happen."

ITUNES EXTRAVAGANZA

Now, a lone filmmaker cannot license directly to, let's say, iTunes. For the most part, even distributors have to go through what is called an "aggregator" to license to a company such as iTunes. An aggregator is a much larger distributor that already has the negotiating deal with these types of platforms. iTunes and other digital market companies do not have the resources or band-width to deal with *individual* filmmakers. They are looking for companies offering at least 100 hours worth of content. So un-less you've spent the last thirty years of your life making at least 400 short films, start looking for a distributor/aggregator if you want to be on iTunes.

One such distributor, the largest short film content provider on iTunes, is Shorts International. Shorts International has a library of over 3000 short films they distribute to not only iTunes, but globally to over 120 broadcasters across every plat-form and every medium. I reached out to Linda Olszewski, who heads up the U.S. acquisitions team here in Los Angeles. Linda had this to say:

"Films play differently on different mediums. So sometimes a film will be a lot more embraced for potential sales if they have more than one cut. Sometimes our licensers are look-ing for a film that's shorter than 15 minutes. So if someone with a 29-minute film would consider doing a couple of dif-ferent cuts, that's always better. On iTunes, it's fine to have a longer cut. And for TV sales you can't sell a film that's be-tween 30 and 40 minutes. They don't have that kind of time in the program. Also, it helps if there's some sort of market-ing angle. At some festivals, it's a negative to have a celeb-rity; for us, it helps. Certain genres are great, like comedy, animation, horror, or experimental work. One of the things that helps us, too, is when the filmmaker designs a really nice cover art. As long as they have really high-res images [resolution], we can create a poster for them. Also, build your fan base. Whether you're doing something on YouTube or MySpace or Facebook, keep that e-mail list going. What's really sad is when you meet a filmmaker who was on the festival circuit, won stuff, and they never ended up doing the work to create their e-mail list. Also, I always tell everybody this—don't be a jerk. When I get two different films and they're similar, and I have someone who's really difficult to deal with and someone who's a gem, I'll always work with the gem. And at this point in the marketplace, I especially want to say that if you shot your short on HD [high definition], your opportunities for TV licensing sale just blossomed. Everything is going to HD, and TV markets are looking at any content that has HD masters, including shorts. It's the first time in U.S. TV licensing that this world is really opening up for shorts, because they need HD content."

BROADCAST LICENSING

One place where you may be able to sidestep this aggregator reality is with television. Often networks that show shorts have film acquisition departments that act like film festival programming teams (like BET [Black Entertainment Network], IFC, Sundance Channel, Logo). You don't need a distributor because they watch stuff like a programmer does and *select* your film for broadcast the way a programmer selects your film for screening at a festival. The downside, of course, is that, like film festivals, many networks get more shorts submitted than they have space to broadcast. But remember—this is filmmaking, people! We are used to making the impossible possible.

SALES AGENTS AND PRODUCER'S REPS

A film representative (at times called a producer's rep) or a sales agent is that person who knows way more than most up-and-coming filmmakers do about the landscape of film sales. While most of you may not need to go this route, they can be very helpful navigating the sometimes scary waters of distribution, particularly if you have a hot film.

Rosie Wong is the Senior Manager of the Sundance Industry

Office. After dealing with hundreds of short and feature film-makers who are looking at distribution options for the first time, she shares this:

> "What I've noticed over the years is that all filmmakers (short and feature length) tend to rely too heavily on outside sources when it comes to distribution. They need to be going into it with a little business and industry savvy, and not just relying on hiring a sales agent or producer's rep. When the sales agent comes to you with a plan for selling your short or a distributor makes you an offer you will already know what they're talking about and can contribute to the overall plan for your film's sale. Empower yourself with information. The next few years will show us a huge expansion of what is available for short film distribution and it will be the filmmakers who educate themselves *now* who will really succeed."

I recently worked with Orly Ravid on the sale of *Happy Birthday*. Even though I am not new to the distribution scene, having someone else negotiate contracts was invaluable. Often, we as artists have difficulty getting what we deserve—a sales agent or film rep can help you do that (without the ulcer). Conversely, there are more direct ways to deal with distributors. Maria Lynn, a longtime champion of indie filmmakers, is the President of Wolfe Releasing (www.wolfereleasing.com). She notes:

> "The experienced people are definitely better for everyone, so find out who they have worked for in the past and talk to their filmmakers. The other alternative is to simply have a lawyer review the terms you've discussed directly with a distributor and get some help with accounting review later on. This allows you to get some personal experience with your distributor. It's important that you trust them; remember, you're going to be working with them a long time."

Orly's "Is Your Film Distribution Ready?" Questionnaire

- Is your music cleared in perpetuity for all rights in all media for the world? If not, you've pretty much ruled yourself out of distribution because unless your short reveals the mysteries of the Universe, no one is going to bother clearing your music for you.

- Are there any images (posters of famous movies, or brands) that are in your film that will pose legal liability to your potential distributor? Be particularly concerned with the degree of visibility and if there is any connotation or messaging that may be inferred regarding the brand that a company might take issue with. Sometimes a filmmaker needs E&O insurance (Errors and Omissions) in order to license shorts in the U.S. to broadcasters, and this will be an issue that can cost you cash (or, worse, a scene you need in your film) when delivering your movie.

- Have you taken good (sexy, provocative, helpful, or intriguing) photography to help market your short film? The availability of a good "hook" image can A. help you get distribution, and B. help your film or compilation sell better on a transactional basis (meaning that if your short is part of a pay-per-view or download-to-own distribution model it will sell better).

- Did you use SAG actors? If so, is your deal with SAG resolved in advance, or is it so punishing that no distributor can take on your film and see a profit, and neither can you?

- What audiences can you target with your film, even if you self-distribute?

continued

- How did you offline your film—if you shot on 35mm and filmed out to 35mm did you also output to HD (Digibeta, BetaSP)? Don't be penny wise and pound foolish by limiting yourself; spend the money to do onlining and outputting and delivery properly so you don't lose opportunities in the future. TV licensing sales blossom if you output to HD.

- Is your short the ideal and perfect running time for itself to adequately tell your story? People often argue shorter is better but that may not always be the case, though it is important that a short not feel too long or too disposable either.

- Did you separate out your music, special effects, and dialogue tracks in your sound mix [DME]? Because some territories dub voices over your film (as opposed to subtitle) and will want to replace your dialogue track with theirs. This is usually more of an issue for features, but as the marketplace globalizes and companies such as Shorts International license to various territories around the world, it's not a bad idea to consider this so you have wider options.

- Do you have the complete script (the film you edited, not your original script) in its original language for easy translation and subtitling? Check out these Web sites for additional info: www.goasa.com or www.wgawregistry.org.

- Do you have a complete music cue sheet in order for your composer to be paid by their publishers (e.g., BMI, ASCAP)?

I couldn't stress the importance of owning your short in its entirety: The script, the music, and making sure *everyone* who graces the screen has signed a document giving you the right to use their "likeness" in perpetuity.

I WOULD LIKE TO THANK THE ACADEMY . . .

Your film is done. You read Orly's Questionnaire and you're ready to send it out to distributors. What's the first thing you should do? Well, if you think (and come on, we all think this) your film has a chance at being short-listed for an Oscar, then the first thing you should do is go online and familiarize yourself with their rules and regulations (www.oscars.org). And read on.

While the Academy regulations may seem daunting, they're actually quite simple. I had lunch with Jon Bloom, who heads up the narrative and animation shorts section. We talked about what constitutes a "qualifying event" in order for a short film-maker to be in a position to submit their film for consideration.

A qualifying event to submit a live-action (narrative) or ani-mated film for Academy consideration includes: a 3-day minimum theater run, and your film must play twice a day (see Fourwall, below); or your short wins a Best Short Film (or Best Animation or Best Documentary) award from a qualifying film festival (check out their Web site for the list). The theater run *must* be in Los Angeles County. For documentary shorts please go to their Web site (www.oscars.com), as the rules will be changing for 2009 and beyond.

Simply put: The Academy Awards are for films that have been theatrically released (at minimum in Los Angeles County) or have been honored as the "Best of" at a qualifying film festival (which to me is, technically, a theatrical release of sorts). Of course this makes sense. The Internet has The Webby Awards, television and cable channels have their awards, and this helps one understand that the Academy Awards are only for *theatri-cally* released films. You freak out—oh my god I've done the fes-tival circuit and haven't won Best Short at any of the qualifying ones! How will I be able to theatrically release my film? It's actu-ally easier than you think.

FOURWALL

"Fourwall" is an old-school industry term that means that you're renting the theater to show your film. Independent features without distribution do this. You might overhear a filmmaker at a festival say, "I fourwalled it and got so-and-so (some big agent or buyer) to come to the screening." If you don't have a film that gets picked up by a distributor for a theatrical release (which is quite improbable for a short), you do it yourself. In days gone by producers hoped to build momentum with press or by attracting agents/managers to show up to the screening. In this case, you are fourwalling your short to qualify for the Academy Awards.

And this, my friend, is considered by Academy standards a theatrical release. See? Easy as pie.

Your film will likely play most at an obscure time slot in the smallest theater. The cost varies, but I do know from negotiating fourwalls for shorts at Sundance that it was somewhere between $250–$350. You approach the booking manager of the theater and ask them if you can pay them to fourwall your film. You think to yourself, "I could get the local theater down the street to let me do it for free!" No, no, you cannot. Remember, the release needs to happen in Los Angeles County (*and* in Manhattan if your short is a documentary—but this may change, so make sure to check out their Web site).

What does this all mean? Well, the Academy doesn't care that iTunes bought your movie, you cannot show your film online *before* you qualify (and this includes your or anybody else's Web site whether people are paying to watch your film or not—it cannot be publicly available online. Period). And they don't care that HBO is presenting your film in a premiere spot just before *The L Word*; you cannot show your film on television *before* you qualify.

And there are two Academy clinchers: Your film has to be *on film*: 16mm, 35mm, or 70mm. So if you shot it digitally you have to transfer (blow-up) your work to film.

This is a critical regulation that you need to think about ahead of time. Transferring to 35mm requires thousands of dollars and a whole lotta headache to accomplish. Now, for the first round (when you first submit your film for consideration) they will accept a 24- or 48-frame progressive scan format with a minimum projector resolution of 2048 by 1080 pixels; source image format conforming to SMPTE 428-1-2006 D-Cinema Distribution Master–Image Characteristics; image compression (if used) conforming to ISO/IEC 15444-1 (JPEG 2000), and image and sound file formats suitable for exhibition in commercial Digital Cinema sites.

Exactly.

Keep this in mind when budgeting post-production if you plan to submit your film for consideration. There are three rounds in the short live action or animation selection process. You can only submit digitally (with the tech specs above) in the *first* round. And the time you'd have to blow up to 16mm, 35mm, or 70mm is somewhere around three weeks from when they tell you you've made it to the next round and when your film has to arrive in their offices. Academy Award–winning documentary filmmaker Cynthia Wade (*Freeheld*), with previous experience, knew what to do:

> "I'd been a cameraperson for the Oscar-nominated short documentary [*The Collector of Bedford Street*, directed by Alice Elliott] and had consulted on the Oscar-nominated feature documentary *Street Fight* [directed by Marshall Curry], so the idea of qualifying the film was a possibility in my mind. It wasn't until *Freeheld* was accepted by 2007 Sundance Film Festival, and won Special Jury Prize there, that we formalized our plan on qualifying the film for Oscar consideration. This meant raising additional funds for the 35mm blow-up and limited theatrical release, and not making a television deal right away. I knew that

streaming the film on the Web could disqualify the film for Oscar consideration, so we opted out of the iTunes offer to make the film available to the public, which many short filmmakers took advantage of at Sundance that year."

And finally let me say this about the Academy Awards and you. Go on Netflix, iTunes, or wherever else you can find them and *watch* what has won in the last few years. If any of those films had a budget of under $40,000 (or even $60,000), I'd be shocked. Also, please consider these submission numbers: 30–40 documentary shorts, 40–60 animation, and 60–100 live action (narrative), and between 3–7 films are nominated. Do your research *before* you think of applying.

CONTRACTS

Honest people use contracts, but you may find some distributors who are not honest. Don't blindly trust anyone, but at the same time, don't waste oodles of dough on a fancy attorney who treats the contract for your tiny short as if it were a mega blockbuster studio picture and gives your distributor notes that are alienating and absurd.

Contrary to popular opinion or assumption, shorter contracts are not better. They just leave more information out, can be vague and unhelpful, and that may leave you having to sue over the omitted information. Because, once you've delivered the master, licenses, and key art, and signed the long form, your film is in the distributor's hands, and let's face it—you're not likely to be able to sue over verbal understanding, so get *everything* in writing. Do NOT assume anything.

One hallmark of integrity of distributors is that they don't ask for exclusive rights *unless* they have the means to exploit them thoroughly. Orly shares:

"More often than not, distributors are very eager to protect their business and sometimes don't think through what they're *really* going to be able to do for the filmmaker, and it's up to the filmmaker to push back and retrieve rights that are not being exploited to their absolute highest potential. Don't be afraid to be confident. If the distributor who owns the rights to your film cannot sell your short to BET but you, the filmmaker, *can* due to your own contacts there, then they *should* want you to be able to do that *without* being in breach of contract. If they don't, you've picked the wrong people."

LITIGATION IS UGLY, PAINFUL, AND EXPENSIVE

Always get a lawyer (or industry person familiar with distribution contracts) to look over any legal documents. You worked hard to get this far so do not, and I really mean it, DO NOT sign anything before you are absolutely certain of what all the terms mean for you and your film's life. The festival and television sales for *Dani and Alice* were handled by Lisa Thrasher, who not only went to law school but was also very patient in explaining each and every section of every contract I signed. Do not be pushed or cajoled into a deal you don't completely understand. I promise you, you will regret it.

WHERE ARE ALL THE DISTRIBUTORS?

One of the most important things about distribution is knowing where to get it. I've included in the Resource Guide at the end of this book a list of distibutors who have been doing this for a long time. However, because this arena is changing constantly, please visit my Web site, www.robertamunroe.com, for an up-to-date list of U.S. and international companies who buy for broadcast and/ or distribute shorts. And also check out the Academy's Web site for a list of qualifying fests and to note any changes that may have happened since the time of this publication: www.oscars.org.

Of course, since it's a recent innovation, digital distribution can be tricky. While Sundance and its distributor, Mediastile, have decided to part ways over a disagreement in royalties, you shouldn't let occasional setbacks like this deter you from utilizing this extraordinary platform to distribute your work. The Sundance Institute will, as it always has, find a way to help filmmakers display their work to the widest possible audience, and I'm certain this bump in the road will be just that, a bump that they will overcome to continue providing short filmmakers with alternative distribution platforms.

I always knew it was possible to get your short film out there with a great chance to monetize it. I haven't made back all the money I spent on *Dani and Alice* or *Happy Birthday*, but I have accomplished DVD, television, and online distribution deals. And, my friend, you can too.

10

Sundance and the
Film Festival Circuit

A SHORT HISTORY OF SHORT FILM
AT THE SUNDANCE FILM FESTIVAL

I would be remiss if I didn't offer up a little background on how the shorts department at Sundance came to be, since my work there helped provide a lot of what I've learned about short films.

When John Cooper, Director of Programming, Sundance Film Festival and Director of Creative Initiatives, Sundance Institute, first started programming at Sundance in 1989, the shorts department consisted of a lonely box of videotapes sitting off to the side. He was told, "Watch them. See if you can make a program out of it." He did, and the Sundance shorts program was launched.

Cooper, Sundance, and hundreds of filmmakers lucked out in 1989, as the likes of Todd Haynes, Alexander Payne, and David O. Russell were in that lonely box.

Cooper convinced agents at the larger talent agencies to come to the shorts program, which provided those filmmakers with the audience that could jump-start their careers. By 1999 Cooper, after watching over a thousand shorts submissions annually, passed the torch to Senior Programmer Trevor Groth.

ONLINE FILM FESTIVAL

Cooper explained to me how the dot-com extravaganza truly pushed short film forward by way of providing a medium for the message. Then, as we all saw, the dot-com arena bottomed out. Now the Internet needed content—free content—and this provided Sundance programmers the opportunity to ramp up short film exposure both at the fest and online. Under the powerhouse energies of Joseph (Joe) Beyer, John Cooper, and the rest of the programming team, the Sundance Online Film Festival became an instant success.

Initially, shorts that played online were selected by Senior Programmers Shari Frilot and Trevor Groth *exclusively* for online viewing, not to screen in the festival live. That quickly changed and the selections from the larger pool were screened live (in Park City and Salt Lake City) by the shorts programmers (Mike Plante and myself) and Trevor Groth. In the beginning, Joe researched and found top-notch partners and other technological support groups that took a filmmaker's master, encoded it (with unbelievable precision), and uploaded it to a masterfully designed Web page. Now filmmakers could enjoy an audience of not just the several hundred people at the festival, but hundreds of thousands worldwide. Now, in partnership with iTunes, every short filmmaker selected for Sundance has the opportunity to be part of the digital revolution. And for the global audience, for $1.99 per download, you could watch most short films that were playing at Sundance pretty much *while* they were playing at Sundance.

In its first year there were 10,000 downloads and by 2006 that number jumped to over 1 million. In 2008 it was an astounding 2.5 million streams served from www.sundance.org. Joe Beyer shares:

"I think it was a perfect storm of a moment in time that first year we served up the same short film program as the Festival in Park City, it was a 'Duh' moment . . . like, why hadn't we done this sooner? The first five years, all we dealt with was video quality issues with filmmakers who were scared about the 'look and feel' of the video, and why not? It wasn't that great in the beginning. Boom, Flash Video came along and now all we respond to are filmmakers who want larger and wider online exposure. All this happened literally overnight. What probably moved us most was seeing the shift completed, seeing the power truly turn away from the establishment and into this independent realm. We always noted while it was happening that it was probably the single most exciting time to be working in shorts. It wasn't that easy to be playing this game in the beginning, but our whole programming team was behind it, and that made all the difference to getting it out there and getting it done for the filmmakers. From the moment I was hired at Sundance it was clear to me that this was a programming team that truly believed in the short form and we all did everything to bring short films into the forefront."

Which leads me to . . .

WHY YOU SHOULDN'T CARE IF YOUR FILM GETS INTO SUNDANCE

I know. You're thinking I'm crazy to tell you not to worry about getting your film into what is considered the Holy Grail of film festivals. Not at all. Even when I was programming at Sundance I was always telling filmmakers this very salient fact: If less than 2% of all submissions are selected in the shorts department, does that mean *every one* of the 98% that weren't chosen was bad? Of course not. Many filmmakers I talk to think that if they

don't get into Sundance their career (the one they're just starting) is over. That's ridiculous. There are hundreds of film festivals all over the world where your short would receive exceptional
exposure (sometimes greater than at Sundance, where the press
and industry folk tend to be focused on features). [John] Cooper
shares:

> "If you don't get into Sundance, don't give up. Treat yourself
> with respect. Keep hold of that self-respect and see if you
> can go to the mid-level, or the regional level festivals. People
> who go to mid-level film festivals can still be discovered. You
> don't need *everybody* to adore you. You need one person to
> believe in you who has money or power to take you to the
> next step, and that's *all* it takes."

While they might exist, I do not know a more prolific filmmaker
than Kevin Everson. He's made three features and more than
fifty short films *in twelve years*. His films have screened at such
prestigious fests as Berlinale, Rotterdam, Sundance, and been
included in galleries all over the world (MOMA, Wurttenbergi-
scher Kunstverein, Stuttgart, Germany, the Whitney). And when
he's not making films he's teaching students how to make them
as an Associate Professor of Art at the University of Viginia.
Kevin breaks down how he looks at getting into Sundance or
not:

> "Sure, it does make your year. But we're [experimental film-
> makers] gutter filmmakers. We're avant-gutter [laughs],
> we're happy to show our films *anywhere*. I have about three
> shorts a year, so either one of those will get into Sundance
> and another will get into somewhere else like Rotterdam. I
> just keep makin' 'em and you all keep showin' 'em [laughs].
> People can say, 'Oh hell, he's a Sundance filmmaker . . ."
> [laughs]. I always push stuff at Sundance because I know

you guys, and you've been supportive, but forget about the Hollywood hype bullshit at Sundance, because to me, it's just like being in the New York Underground. It's the same shit I see all year long. It starts at Sundance and it ends in Texas [at Cinematexas Film Festival]. Just get your work out there and it'll all take care of itself."

Think about it. If your film gets into a smaller festival, the local press is very supportive of it and they want to talk to all the film-makers. A festival where you can be a big fish in a small pond, maybe even win an award or two along the way, have the time and space to beef up your filmmaker network, and grab audi-ence e-mails (remember what Tiffany said, "Your e-mail list is your gold."). While I was in New York City recently, I had the pleasure to meet with Denise Kassell. Denise was the director of the Hampton Film Festival for six years, and is a well respected programmer and film festival consultant (www.filmfestconsult ing.com). Denise was happy to share her wisdom:

"I think it depends on what your mission is. At Sundance, especially in terms of shorts, the programmers can get any films they want. Because they have that reputation and everybody goes there and it's a magnet, the grande dame of cinema. The question is, why are we making and distribut-ing films? It's the same thing in terms of political action: Do you always preach to the converted? Will it have an effect? Or do you preach to the unconverted, and will that give you a greater effect? I think it does. So in terms of personal work, getting shorts out to the communities, there's some-thing very rewarding about having a small effect or a re-gional effect, and getting people that would not necessarily see these films to see these films. Also, the little gem is maybe overlooked at a bigger festival, because they think it's so far beyond them that they never even get there. So there's something that happens on a regional level or a local level, and these people don't even think of going to Sundance, and that's an amazing service to be doing for the public. And for the filmmaker."

While Sundance is seen as the most prestigious domestic festival for short filmmakers, outside of the U.S. it's Clermont-Ferrand. CF happens every February in Clermont-Ferrand, France. Their market is attended by some of the top buyers, distributors, and festival programmers internationally. There is no entry fee; they show approximately 190 films, of which fewer than 25 come from North America. The average number of submissions they receive is close to 6,000 (1,200 French and 4,800 international)—a bit more than Sundance. Laurent Crouzeix has programmed for CF for over ten years. He gives us an overview:

"We have three competitions and there is a selection committee of about ten people for each. The films are shared between groups of two programmers who view the films. This means that each film submitted to Clermont-Ferrand is seen by at least two programmers. All the films that have been viewed by all members of the committee are then discussed to choose the ones that are going to be selected. It is a very democratic process. Some choices are easy, but for others discussions can become tense. The organization of the festival rests on collective decision, and so does the selection. For international entries, less than 10% of the films submitted make it to the final round of discussions. Yet a number of films that may not make it to the selection can actually be picked up for other programs, like children's programs for instance. Some eventually make it to a special thematic or regional retrospective years later. You never know . . ."

But what I think is one of the best things about Clermont-Ferrand for filmmakers is their incredible market. Whether you are selected for their festival or not, your film is uploaded into their digital marketplace. Rows of computers are available for anyone to view your film during the festival. You are given the opportunity to target buyers or programmers you know will be in attendance to watch your film at the market—it's an opportunity not to be missed.

Other notable short film festivals that are outstanding are Oberhausen (Germany), Ottawa International Animation Festival, and the São Paulo Short Film Festival (Brazil). These are festivals that step way outside the mainstream box while still programming mainstream work. For experimental filmmakers these festivals (and there are many others—you gotta sign up with Withoutabox!) offer a world of choices.

SUBMISSIONS—PLEASE, LOSE THE HIGH-TECH DVD CASE

The first thing every smart filmmaker does is register at www.withoutabox.com, which is an awesome site dedicated to independent filmmakers and the festivals that showcase them. And every first-time filmmaker I've talked to over the years stresses about what the festival programmers think: about their DVD case, their glossy cover photograph, their professional-looking poster-style credits, and their exquisitely worded press release on the back flap.

Please. At the larger festivals (like Sundance) nobody sees that stuff except the submissions department, and they don't care. Your DVD case is opened and put into DVD cases that hold around 200 DVDs each and *then* it is sent out to the shorts programmers along with 199 other hopefuls. After the programmers have watched it, it is returned to your expensive DVD case and shelved until decisions are made. Adam Montgomery,

Programming Department Manager at Sundance Film Festival, notes:

> "Sometimes it actually makes me kind of sad to see people go through all of the effort of making fancy packaging and including an elaborate paper press kit. With 9,000 submissions [this number includes feature films], there simply isn't time for us to look over all of that stuff. In most cases, everything but the DVD itself is immediately recycled or discarded. The best kind of submission comes in an easy-to-open bubble mailer that contains only a DVD with the film title and tracking number clearly written on the case AND on the face of the disc."

Often, at Sundance, filmmakers would also send in elaborate and expensive press kits. I promise you, Mike [Plante] and I never even saw that stuff before we watched your film *and more importantly* we didn't see it *before* we made our decisions on what to select. And while it would sound more official if I told you that we wanted to keep our decision-making process free from influence, it also boiled down to the fact that we simply didn't have time while watching more than five thousand films in four months. The same goes for DVD menus and front credits sequences. Don't do it. Kim Yutani, Sundance Short Film Programmer, tells it straight up:

> "A lot of times I try not to look at the title or notice who has made it, because I want to come at it with as clear and unbiased a frame of mind that I could possibly be in. And I pop it in, and I get a menu screen with all sorts of shit on there, like special features, outtakes, director's commentary— you're wasting my time. I have to figure out *how* to play your movie, and now I'm mad. Anything that takes me out of my path of watching somebody's film is distracting. And there's

one huge mistake that filmmakers make, and that's trying to impress you with all these doohickeys that they don't need. The same for front credits. Filmmakers don't seem to understand that lengthy front credits just make your film seem too long. I love it if I can just pop it in the DVD player and I get to *immediately* start watching your film. I can *immediately* get into the story you're trying to tell."

The one thing I *would* suggest you do: Fill out your submission form *completely*. If you want a programmer to know something about your film's career that you feel is pertinent—like it won Best Short at the Nashville LGBT Film Festival—make sure to include that in the Previous Screening field on your submission form. Because while we may not have time to track down your press kit, programmers do go into the submissions database from time to time to see where the film has played previously.

ADAM MONTGOMERY'S SUBMISSION DO'S AND DON'TS

- Do complete the submission form in its entirety.
- Don't send small animals as gifts.
- Do send chocolates or scotch.
- Don't package your work so it takes four people and vise grips to get it open.
- Do make sure that your DVD plays all the way through before mailing it in.
- Don't use paper labels on your DVD. They are the leading cause of unplayable discs.
- Do write or print your film title and tracking number directly on the face of the disc with a **black Magic Marker.**
- Don't include promotional items from your film. They will be discarded unless they are *really* clever.

- Do familiarize yourself with the festival's rules and eligibility requirements *before* filling out the application.
- Don't send in a new cut of your film without asking first—it will only cause confusion!
- Don't shrink-wrap your DVD case. It won't make your film look any more professional or legitimate.
- Don't send in a VHS tape—nobody wants to dust off the old VCR just because you couldn't figure out how to burn a DVD. [But if that's all you have access to—send it in.]
- Do be patient. Calling to plead your case will only make you look desperate. Let your work speak for itself.

One other thing you may want to look into when submitting your film to a festival is uploading your film to an ftp site (File Transfer Protocol). This year I started sending out my ftp site for programmers to watch my film by streaming it from the site itself without the need to download it onto their systems or stream it off my site. If I can upload my film, anyone can. It saves me (and the environment) postage, eliminates the possibility of lost DVDs, and gives programmers instant access to my work. Even Clermont-Ferrand is offering this service to filmmakers who have participated in the festival or in the market. Once you've been selected at festivals like Sundance you are given your own folder on their ftp site to upload photos and press kits.

You may feel a little old-fashioned about this. You want your film to be seen in the best possible way, but I can assure you many programmers are watching your film on their laptop anyway. Not all festivals have the infrastructure to download your film from your ftp site but if they do, take advantage of it. Do a Web search for ftp client sites, remembering this *is* the Internet, so make sure your file sharing is done with a secure site.

SUBMISSION FEES

By now, you've done your research and know which festivals you want to submit to. You have a small budget (Right? You did put in a budget line *before* you started making your film for marketing and festival submissions—right?). Where does a short filmmaker begin?

Here's something to keep in mind: Many festivals outside the United States (and a few within) do not charge a submission fee. Do some research on which fests screen your type of work and *apply there first*. Also keep in mind that once your film screens at a prominent U.S. festival, many programmers will solicit your film for submission, waiving the fee. What also happens is that because a programmer (with the power to invite your film on the spot) sees it at a festival and invites you to screen at their festival you don't even have to submit it except to send them a DVD for their library or marketplace. It could happen.

Every festival has some flexibility around submission fees. However, understand that it is usually submission fees that help pay for a significant chunk of submission department costs (particularly at smaller festivals with little or no corporate sponsorship), so I encourage you to pay full price to submit to the smaller fests. And then you can focus your begging and pleading energies on requesting waivers *early* from larger festivals, because you may get lucky and get the fee waived before they've reached their fee waiver quotas. There are definitely some festivals that never waive fees, so make sure you have money left over in your post budget for these expenses.

RENTAL FEES

There are a few festivals (most in the lesbian and gay, women's, and genre-specific fests) that will pay you a rental fee for your film. For *Dani and Alice* the official rental fee was $350 per festival. However, for the most part they usually pay somewhere between $100–$250. Some festivals will ask you to forgo the rental fee and instead offer you a flight and/or accommodations. Take them up on their offer! Better you have an opportunity to promote yourself and your film (and your next film) than a few hundred dollars in your pocket. Unless of course you find yourself homeless after post-production; then by all means insist on a rental fee and go get yourself a meal.

OUCH, THAT HURT

There isn't a filmmaker in the world—and I mean in the *entire world*—who has not received his fair share of rejection letters. I remember laughing with Mark and Jay Duplass about how many rejection letters *This Is John* received after premiering at Sundance. I think that that film played at another maybe four or five festivals before they couldn't take it any more and stopped submitting it further.

So it is here that I will outline why a film gets rejected from a festival:

- It's not good.
- It's good but too long.
- It's good but too short.
- It's good but there isn't room in the program for it.
- It's got big-name actors.
- It doesn't have big-name actors.
- It's good but came in too late (you missed the deadline or they've already gone to print with their catalog).
- It's good but came in too early (before the programming staff even start and the year-round receptionist put it in his drawer and forgot to give it to someone).

- It's good but not for this particular festival (you made a live-action mockumentary and sent it to an animation festival).
- It was a rough cut that was a little too rough.
- You didn't pay the submission fee (yes, some fests won't even watch your film if you didn't send a check).

You've heard this before—many really really great films do not get programmed. There is only so much room in a ninety-minute program, and that often leaves great work left on the board. I cannot tell you how many times I had to accept that a wonderful short wasn't going to make the final cut. Once, a really sweet hand-drawn (my favorite kind of animated work) animation was one of my top picks. Mike, Trevor, and I kept that card on the board until the final moment when we agreed there just wasn't room for it. I went outside, called a friend, smoked a cigarette, and cried. Yes, even the programmers watching your film get emotional when it doesn't make the cut.

Finally, I've got to say, the most ridiculous reason some (usually not that good to begin with) filmmakers *think* their film didn't get selected:

- You don't know me, you didn't send me a bottle of scotch, you aren't sleeping with me or with someone who *is* sleeping with me, or your film is too close in storyline to my friend's film that I did select.

Notwithstanding the fact that it would have been physically impossible for me to sleep with every short filmmaker I've programmed, it is just insane to suggest that *all* the programmers at *all* the festivals you were rejected from are acting without integrity when making film selections—particularly those under such scrutiny as Sundance. Believe me when I tell you I have actually lost so-called friends when I made that "Sorry we couldn't find a spot for your film" call. And, for the record, I live in Los Angeles, California. The city where everyone *acts* like your best friend so it would *appear* as though I am friends with all the people I've programmed—but it just ain't so.

OKAY, SO WHERE SHOULD I SUBMIT MY FILM FIRST?

There is a ton of information on film festivals out there. There are a few places I would start (e.g., www.filmfestivals.com). As I mentioned earlier, subscribe to www.withoutabox.com, then go online and do a search for "film festival lists," where you can begin looking at www.filmfestivals.com, and then go out and buy Chris Gore's book *The Ultimate Film Festival Survival Guide*. I want you to go out and buy that book to use as a reference alongside your withoutabox subscription *before* you start submitting to festivals. And I want you to take that book off the shelf and read through it after you receive your rejection letter from Sundance—I know, god forbid you should be one of the 5,400 filmmakers to receive one but, hey, it could happen. And I want you to be prepared and know where to turn next if it does.

PREMIERES–CAN I PLAY IN DETROIT *AND* FLINT, MICHIGAN?

There isn't a programmer alive who can convince me that having a premiere regulation (where your film cannot have played *anywhere* prior to their festival) for short films is a good idea. It's not required at Sundance or Clermont-Ferrand. Laurent at Clermont-Ferrand tells it like it is:

> "Premieres for shorts is a perfect example of duplicating the environment of feature films at festivals and applying it to shorts—and that is totally absurd. Big A-list festivals

sometimes tend to do so. I always ask their representatives what is the point in requesting a premiere for a short. The answer is invariably the same: because we're a big festival. I never heard one good reason that could justify such a silly practice. Premieres are nothing but an obstacle to the free circulation of films and the free access of festival audiences to films. Everyone knows that exhibition opportunities are very limited for shorts. No one claiming to support short film can sensibly apply this kind of premiere rule. The role of festivals is to bring together films and audiences, not to restrict opportunities for short films of being seen. Do the Olympics require that participants have never competed in another sports competition before? No. Why? Because it wouldn't make any sense. The festival circuit is often acting as a training ground for filmmakers to develop their craft and expose their work to audiences. Let them enjoy as many opportunities to screen their film as possible."

Well said! However, it is my duty to inform you that some festivals indeed require your film to be a premiere (either in that country or sometimes just the city the festival is in), so please do your homework so you can decide which festivals are worth holding out for.

OH MY GOD! I GOT IN!

Ah, the sweet smell of success! You finally got the letter that begins, "We are pleased to inform you . . ." Sweet! Now what do you do? Well, things are different for every festival, so talk to the Hospitality Coordinator/Guest Services person in order to prepare to attend your film's screening. I reached out to Virginia Pearce, Director of Guest Services at Sundance. She's been helping filmmakers, producers, special guests, and industry folk for ten years at one of the most stressful festivals in the world. She offers some advice on how to get on the Good Karma List:

- Be kind to festival staff and volunteers and they will reward you well—we know you're crazed and nervous *and* excited and we *want* to help you have a great experience. It's our job!
- Get things in on time. This will change your life. If we have all the information necessary to promote your work at the festival, your time gathering all the required documents will be well worth it. You don't want to be spending $400 at the local copy shop on opening night because you didn't get everything to us on deadline.
- Come for as long as you can afford to. Festivals can be expensive, but the people you meet, the films you see, and the feedback you get on your film is an experience you can't replicate.
- See films—many a filmmaker has rued the day they spent their whole time doing business. Carve out some time to see films, check out a panel, or hang out at the filmmaker lounge.
- Bring friends—festivals can be lonely places; bring some friends who can help pass out flyers, hang posters, and provide a shoulder to laugh/cry on.
- Use the festival staff *during* the festival. We are here to help and sometimes don't have much contact with filmmakers during the festival once they check in. We usually have extra tickets to things like screenings or parties; we've got great tips of what/where/when to go places, and are eager to share.
- Drink a lot of water, carry breath mints, and don't worry if you throw up on the first day . . . it happens a lot.

I would add:

- Don't be late for your screening.
- Always acknowledge the other filmmakers in your program.
- Try to remember who to thank, and if you are too nervous, write it down.
- If you are the filmmaker being asked most of the questions during a Q & A, ask your own question of one of the other filmmakers on stage with you.
- Never disparage another filmmaker's work—you think you're whispering, but there is always a chance someone will overhear you and you'll look like a jerk.
- Keep a pen and paper handy! Many people do not carry business cards and you want to get their e-mail addresses.

Film festivals are magical places. You get to watch your film with an audience (!), hear their thoughts in Q & A sessions, meet other filmmakers, and be one of them. Go to as many festivals as you can afford to! Campbell Ex (www.blackmanvision.com), an experimental and documentary filmmaker who works out of the UK, shares that while he isn't the most "schmoozy" person, he does make the most of film festivals whenever possible:

"Festivals seem to increase my contacts with other filmmakers and audience members and enable me to have an international audience that is very important to me. I usually make cards to hand to people. Then usually forget to give them out [laughs]. I keep in touch with people I genuinely click with rather than thinking they could be useful to my career. My advice is to do everything you can to make sure people see it at film festivals, parties, galleries, online. Check out distributors who might be interested in your type of film and invite them. Develop a relationship with people even if nothing comes out of it that first time."

WHY IS MY ANIMATION SCREENING WITH A DOCUMENTARY?

There hasn't been a single festival I've programmed where a filmmaker didn't come up and ask me why their film was programmed in that particular program. I could write a seventy-page dissertation on how programs are put together, so I've reached out to a couple of programmers. Basil Tskiokos, Director of New-Fest (www.newfest.org), and U.S. Sundance Documentary Feature Programming Associate, sheds some light on the situation:

"Mixed genre programs often just don't work. Though there are exceptions—animation, experimental, and often documentary mixed programs can be quite successful. One thing we try not to do unless there's a really good reason or unless the films themselves fit amazingly well together, is to do racially segregated programming—i.e., all black gay films, or all Asian lesbian films. Depending on how this is done, it can send the inadvertent message that these films are not 'for' anyone but solely for the targeted community of color, and that is extremely limiting."

And Bill Guntzler, Director of the Cleveland International Film Festival (one of my favorite festivals in the world), adds:

"I wouldn't say that there is an exact 'science' of programming shorts. Though, there is definitely a sort of intuition a programmer (short or otherwise) needs to build a well-rounded program. While we don't necessarily program thematically, we do want all the short films within a program to complement each other, we love it when we're able to create a short-film program that is 'more than the sum of its parts' where each film adds something to a larger narrative. What we try to create most is a program that has many different elements of filmmaking. A 'dream' program for our festival would have each of the following: a narrative film, a documentary film, an animated film, an experimental film, and a student film. We also have many awards for short films and we like to 'spread the wealth' in that at least every category of award is represented by a film in each program. We especially like a program that will make the audience laugh, cry, be shocked, and be challenged. When we're able to create a program that is a mix of all these elements and we have an appreciative audience (either raving about the films or questioning the films) we know we've done a good job."

And there are also many filmmakers I spoke with who found festivals truly a place to rest—regardless of where their film was placed, and in some instances, especially because of where their film was placed. Deanna Bowen (www.deannabowen.ca) is a Toronto-based media installation artist. Her work has been exhibited in Canada (Ontario, British Columbia, Yukon Territories, Manitoba) and internationally (Germany, France, Switzerland, Italy) in numerous film festivals and galleries. She loves the way festivals have programmed her work and shares:

"The festival scene *was* the scene when I started making work. Gallery installations with film/video were happening, but not quite to the extent that we're used to today, so festivals were the place to go. When I started getting accepted into festivals I was surprised since my works are these dark conceptual/autobiographical pieces that often defy description, not being traditional experimental cinema and not quite traditional gallery material. Getting accepted gave me an enormous amount of confidence and helped me to believe that I could actually make a life out of making moving images. My first video work, *sadomasochism*, got picked up by the Oberhausen festival in Germany and I have to say it was one of the most amazing experiences to have had as a novice maker. I learned so much about my own work by looking at the work of others and those experiences contributed to *sadomasochism's* presentation as a full-scale installation. The opportunity to place my work within an international conversation was such an important thing for me, and the success of that work had a huge impact on how people perceived the videos that followed. Naturally, I can only gush about the fantastic opportunities that arise out of the festival experience. The fresh discussions that are emerging out of experimental festivals about what constitutes a moving image, ideas of cinema as sculpture and/or the role of the artist/maker are really exciting! The flow between the festival and the gallery gets easier, and with that the conversations between experimental moving image makers is becoming increasingly challenging—in all the right ways! Who wouldn't want to be a part of that???"

TO FILM SCHOOL OR NOT TO FILM SCHOOL

There are so many truly great film schools in the world, from the Sam Spiegel Film & Television School in Israel to NYU Tisch School of the Arts to the New York Film Academy to North Carolina to UCLA and USC here in Los Angeles. I have seen (and programmed) so many great films from film schools I'd be hard pressed to advise you not to consider it.

But if school isn't your thing and you want to just get out there and make a film, I can tell you that from what I've seen on the festival circuit and within the film industry in general, film school is not a prerequisite to being successful. Take a look at the bios of filmmakers who have had their films selected at top-tier film festivals and you will see that many did not go to film school. Denise Kassell echoes what I heard from many film school alumni:

"This is not going to be a popular statement, but American youth are coddled more than any other teens else where in the world. There are many people going to the best film schools that are being paid for by their parents or grandparents, so they feel a sense of entitlement and it carries through to graduate school. The awards that are given in film schools are *nothing* like the real world. Quite frankly, they are unprepared for the film business. It is a *business*. There is the world of making art shorts, but even *that* is a business. These art curators still have to answer to the board [of directors]. So all along the way, America is a bottom-line country. Sooner or later, somebody has to pay. And that is something that is not really taught in film school."

I'll also share that there were three words on a ratings sheet in the shorts department at Sundance that were all I needed to read: "bad film school." It told me that the script was "safe" (boy meets girl, all the characters are under the age of ten, senior citizens find love, etc.), the camera was in the right place, but wasn't unique or interesting, the performances were stilted, the lighting looked like you were still studying Lighting 101, and worst of all it was 20 minutes long when 10 would have been more than sufficient to tell the story. Oh, and out of nowhere, there was a crane shot in it. And, I understand that at your school, your film *has to be* 20 minutes long in order for you to receive a passing grade, but is that the cut of the film you think you should submit to Sundance?

No, not all film school work looks like this (some were the best of what was submitted)—I'm only describing the bad ones.

I asked Kim Yutani, Sundance Film Festival Shorts Programmer, for her thoughts:

"One of the things I want to say about film school is that I'm not anti–film school, and the schools that really separate themselves from other schools are the ones stressing *story*. They're not just training their filmmakers to make studio films or commercials, and that shows. If I can tell that something is a student film, and the story is just different, I might think, 'I wonder if this is a Columbia short? Or a film from North Carolina [School of the Arts]?' [In 2008] at Sundance there were easily twelve Columbia shorts that we could have taken. It was because the stories were interesting and original, and the acting was good, the direction was really strong. After you watch 5,000 or so shorts [laughs] you really start to see pieces where the stories are repetitive. So many people will take a very mainstream or film school approach. And there is a way you can tell that story differently, whether it's different visually, or going out on a limb and taking a different path creatively. If you're thinking about attending film school do some research to see who is graduating truly talented filmmakers."

And, of course, I have spoken to several successful filmmakers for whom film school was the best thing they could have done for their careers. We've all heard, and it's true, that there are definitely perks to graduating from certain film schools because not only can it give you a leg up in the industry through contacts and alumni, going to film school also provides you with two major bonuses—technical skills that create a solid foundation for your future work and, most important, community.

Every filmmaker I spoke with who went to film school still works with their fellow graduates in some capacity. Will Speck and Josh Gordon went to film school together in New York and have worked together ever since. From film school shorts (*Culture*) to those amazing Geico commercials (*Caveman*, *Gekko*) to co-directing *Blades of Glory* (written by Jeff and Craig Cox) that starred Will Ferrell and Jon Heder (of *Napoleon Dynamite* fame), Will and Josh's partnership is a testament to developing your filmmaker community. Will discusses the value of both choosing the film school route and diving directly into the industry:

> "One of the differences between filmmakers who have gone to film school and those who haven't is not seeing a lot of shorts and not being in a community of other people who are producing shorts. At film school, I helped film, I acted in them, I produced them, and each one is a learning curve. It's probably hard, especially within the context of what a short film should be, to get a sense of that if you're not around other people who are dealing with it. Though there is an illusion that happens in film school, sort of making the film in your basement and showing it and the world will open up to you. We did that the first time in school, and it didn't really get out too much. It was better to get a job, make some connections, and then when the film was ready, take advantage of the people that we had already met. You're in a position where you're not blindly calling people."

PUBLICITY AND MARKETING

Up-and-coming filmmakers tend to go overboard when it comes to marketing their film. Posters, press kits, flyers, postcards, and press releases blanket the festival and surrounding city. I always thought it was a rather expensive way to alert people that, yes, you had made a movie! I reached out to Jim Dobson, owner of Indie PR in Los Angeles. Jim has worked with many filmmakers and celebrities (Merchant/Ivory, Franco Zeffirelli, et al.) and worked on countless films, film festivals, and film events. Jim shares this advice for the new-to-the-scene short filmmaker:

"The days of marketing through postcards and flyers are really over for most filmmakers. With the advent of online promotion there are so many new avenues to reach the public in regards to your film. The best advice is to create a compelling e-mail blast which includes either an embedded trailer of the short or a direct link to the trailer and Web site. Also include detailed information on the screening dates, locations and times and if anyone will be present from the film. Facebook is one of the best outlets for promotion since you can target regional areas, ages, and niche markets much easier and the response is greater than with MySpace and other outlets. The most important advice of all is to make sure you have plenty of high-quality images for your short, as that will put you ahead of the pack in terms of getting press notice and compelling interest from viewers. Too many filmmakers do not focus on this very simple element and when they are finished with the film it is too late to go back and pull a clean image from the print. Also, do not worry about a glamorous press kit or Web site; always remember to stick to the facts, make it compelling and interesting through the use of photos and video, and people will want to check it out."

Another marketing aspect that many filmmakers overlook is where they choose to screen their film on the festival circuit. Earlier I mentioned the festivals that have premiere regulations, but you, the filmmaker, can also begin thinking about your premiere regulations. Jonathon Aubrey, Vice President of Theatrical Marketing of Regent Releasing, advises:

"One of the most important aspects of any film marketing campaign includes festival placement, and for short films this should be no different. In some ways, festival placement is the first part of any marketing campaign because it is often the first place your film meets an audience and where there is potential for press, distributor interest, and word of mouth/buzz creation. Filmmakers should take time to research all festivals and strategize their submissions accordingly. What are the kinds of films that have played there and been successful? Who are the filmmakers who made success from their screenings at this festival and how? They should ask themselves these questions and think about where their film might play best and how that screening can help them to get to the next level whether it be the next festival, the next screening, or the next film."

As you've learned throughout this book, a robust Web site alongside a stellar collection of still photographs, and a simple business card directing people to your Web site is all you really need in terms of marketing and publicity. Learning the value of video streaming online may not only upgrade your Web site, but may also help find you some work!

Diana Sargant Gibson is a marketing maverick and philanthropist. She has done a significant amount of Web site design research, since she runs a high net worth sales company and charity Web site (www.charitysupporters.com). Diana gives us some advice:

"If you've got a Web site you absolutely should be posting at least a trailer of your short film on it. When businesses optimize their Web sites with video content, its ranking [on search engines like Google] is greatly enhanced. It's safe to assume that retailers and manufacturers will be running—not walking—to make videos to satisfy the appetite of the hungry consumer. Which is where the short filmmaker comes in. So, if you're looking for work while you're waiting for your career to take off, know that consumers are not just watching movies. They are watching 'how to' videos, product demos, and other videos that have been put together for the sole purpose of offering more information to the consumer about a product or a service. For example, I recently met with one of my small business customers (a martial arts instructor) and he showed me seven videos he had recently made of one of his students breaking boards. He wanted advice from me about how he could make them a 'little fancier' or 'polished' so he could post them on his Web site and on YouTube. I teamed him up with a filmmaker I knew and together they were able to create videos that significantly increased his business."

Whether you're a professional, novice, or home-video filmmaker, there is a place for you and your work to shine. It can be on YouTube, at your mom's sixtieth birthday, on Kari's Karate School's Web site, or at the Sundance Film Festival.

The possibilities are endless.

11

It's Time to Make Magic

After fifteen years of programming film, two years of writing, 100 cartons of cigarettes, several cases of scotch, and thousands of hours combing the world for the best of the best (not to mention the many late-night therapy appointments)—I realized there is one thing I couldn't possibly provide you with within the confines of this book.

Faith.

Faith in your ability to accomplish a great short film can only come from within. But, if I may, I'd like to share that the greatest filmmakers in the history of filmmaking all had their moments of sheer terror. I myself have first-hand knowledge of that churning feeling in my stomach as I've approached a brand-new journey—whether it was starting a new job, making a film, or even writing this book. With knowledge and development of that Big Belief Place, you will overcome it. I promise you that.

During the writing and editing of this book, I had a

conversation with Lorna Ruud (my friend Dennis's mom). We were laughing about all the crazy things we did when we were young and she said, "You never know more than you do when you're twenty." I'd like to echo that with regard to you and me and this book:

> You never know more about filmmaking than when you make your first film.

It's a magical time—the making of your first film. This is not the time to beat yourself up over what you don't know. Or to be overzealous with what you *think* you *do* know. This is the time to truly cultivate your style and celebrate your voice.

No one can make the film you can. No one. So get out there and make it.

We're waiting for you.

Steak and Dominic's Budgets

Steak and Dominic's DIY 11k
"Your lead actor is also your DP"

Producer: Your Girlfriend
Writer: You
Director: You

Acct No	Category Description
1100	STORY & RIGHTS
1200	PRODUCERS UNIT
1300	DIRECTION
1400	CAST
1500	ATL TRAVEL
	TOTAL ABOVE-THE-LINE
2000	PRODUCTION
2200	ART DEPARTMENT
2500	SET OPERATIONS
2900	WARDROBE
3100	MAKE-UP & HAIRDRESSING
3200	SET LIGHTING
3300	CAMERA
3400	PRODUCTION SOUND
3500	TRANSPORTATION
3600	LOCATIONS/FOOD
3700	HARD DRIVES/TAPE STOCK
	TOTAL PRODUCTION
4500	POST PRODUCTION
	TOTAL POST PRODUCTION
6700	INSURANCE
6800	LLC FEES
6900	SAG BOND
	Contingency / L&D
	TOTAL OTHER
	Total Above-The-Line
	Total Below-The-Line
	Total Above and Below-The-Line
	Grand Total

Budget created by Steak House and Dominic Ottersbach - Steakhaus Productions, LLC

Shoot Dates: This Weekend
Total Shoot Days: 2
Unions: SAG Shortcut
Location: Your Apartment

	Page	Total
	1	0
	1	0
	1	0
	1	0
	1	0
		0
	2	0
	2	500
	2	1,050
	3	200
	3	0
	3	550
	4	1,025
	4	325
	5	1,400
	5	1,200
	5	350
		6,600
	7	3,100
		3,100
	8	300
	8	0
	8	0
		1,000
		1,300
		0
		11,000
		11,000
		11,000

Steak and Dominic's 18k Bonanza
"You're driving the Grip Truck!"

Producers: Your Ex-Best Friend
Writers: You
Director: You

Acct No	Category Description
1100	STORY & RIGHTS
1200	PRODUCERS UNIT
1300	DIRECTION
1400	CAST
1500	ATL TRAVEL
	TOTAL ABOVE-THE-LINE
2000	PRODUCTION
2200	ART DEPARTMENT
2500	SET OPERATIONS
2900	WARDROBE
3100	MAKE-UP & HAIRDRESSING
3200	SET LIGHTING
3300	CAMERA
3400	PRODUCTION SOUND
3500	TRANSPORTATION
3600	LOCATIONS/FOOD
3700	HARD DRIVES/TAPE STOCK
	TOTAL PRODUCTION
4500	POST PRODUCTION
	TOTAL POST PRODUCTION
6700	INSURANCE
6800	LLC FEES
6900	SAG BOND
	Contingency / L&D
	TOTAL OTHER
	Total Above-The-Line
	Total Below-The-Line
	Total Above and Below-The-Line
	Grand Total

Budget created by Steak House and Dominic Ottersbach - Steakhaus Productions, LLC

Shoot Dates: When the script rocks!
Total Shoot Days: 2
Unions: SAG Shortie
Location: Somewhere you can make a quick getaway

	Page	Total
	1	0
	1	0
	1	0
	1	500
	1	0
		500
	2	1,500
	2	1,300
	2	1,850
	3	600
	3	400
	3	1,350
	4	2,225
	4	725
	5	1,400
	5	950
	5	350
		12,650
	7	3,100
		3,100
	8	300
	8	0
	8	0
		1,655
		1,955
		500
		17,705
		18,205
		18,205

Steak and Dominic's 32k Special
"My Grandma died 'n' left me some money"

Producer: Demanda Tension
Writer: You
Director: You

Acct No	Category Description
1100	STORY & RIGHTS
1200	PRODUCERS UNIT
1300	DIRECTION
1400	CAST
1500	ATL TRAVEL
	TOTAL ABOVE-THE-LINE
2000	PRODUCTION
2200	ART DEPARTMENT
2500	SET OPERATIONS
2900	WARDROBE
3100	MAKE-UP & HAIRDRESSING
3200	SET LIGHTING
3300	CAMERA
3400	PRODUCTION SOUND
3500	TRANSPORTATION
3600	LOCATIONS / FOOD
3700	HARD DRIVES / TAPE STOCK
	TOTAL PRODUCTION
4500	POST PRODUCTION
	TOTAL POST PRODUCTION
6700	INSURANCE
6800	LLC FEES
6900	SAG BOND
	Contingency / L&D
	TOTAL OTHER
	Total Above-The-Line
	Total Below-The-Line
	Total Above and Below-The-Line
	Grand Total

Budget created by Steak House and Dominic Ottersbach - Steakhaus Productions, LLC

Shoot Date: As soon as Grandma dies
Total Shoot Days: 3
Unions: SAG Short Pants
Location: Exotic Location #7

	Page	Total
	1	0
	1	0
	1	0
	1	4,903
	1	0
		4,903
	2	2,500
	2	1,500
	2	2,800
	3	700
	3	600
	3	2,050
	4	3,025
	4	925
	5	2,250
	5	3,450
	5	350
		20,150
	7	3,100
		3,100
	8	900
	8	0
	8	0
		2,905
		3,805
		4,903
		27,055
		31,958
		31,958

Top Short Filmmaker Clichés

Several years ago, Mike Plante (who was my partner in crime, programming shorts at Sundance), after watching several thousand shorts, sent around an e-mail with the top fifty short-film clichés. Many of those are listed below along with others that programmers, filmmakers, and distributors shared with me. Yes, have a laugh—but also *take note*.

- Is there a Japanese tea ritual opening scene?
- Do any of your characters point a gun to their own heads while breathing heavily?
- Is there a woman in your film masturbating to poetry/spoken word?
- Is the female lead avenging a rape?
- Is there a ninja in your film?
- Is the male rapist living through painful remorse that resembles hell on earth metaphorically or via CG?
- Is Deborah Harry in your movie? Alison Janney?
- Does your protagonist drive down a foggy road, all of a sudden seeing a child in a white nightgown who mysteriously disappears on the reverse shot?
- Is your WWII story set in the hills of Griffith Park?

Prospect Park? Palm Springs desert? Appalachian Mountains?

- Does your Black male lead really really *really* want to be a rapper/basketball player?
- Is Jesus Christ in your film? Is he Black?
- Is your film based on a short story by someone far more talented than you are? Joyce Carol Oates? Raymond Carver? Jean-Paul Sartre? Kafka?
- Does your rock-star lead overcome his drug addiction just in time to perform for the record label executives?
- Does your film's score begin with solitary piano? Acoustic guitar? The theme from *The Mission*? *Requiem for a Dream*? *Shaft*?
- Does your DVD menu have more choices than a feature? Does it have tone and color bars? Do I have to scroll through fifteen steps before I can even watch your movie?
- Is the title of your film *Twilight*? *The Good Neighbor*? *Forgiven*?
- Does someone vomit in your film? Does it look like milk and Oreo cookies?
- Is there a convenience-store robbery that goes awry? Are the owners a Korean couple stumbling through broken English?
- Is the reason the robbery goes awry due to the English-as-a-second-language issue?
- Are the robbers Black or Latino men who are actually law-abiding citizens who are in the wrong place at the wrong time?
- Is your film called *One-Night Stand*?
- Are two people sitting in a car talking about nothing? Do we find out they're about to commit a crime? That they're actually dead?

- Is your film about a war (Vietnam, Iraq, Desert Storm, WWI, or WWII)? Is there a scene where the general is reading/writing at an old desk, looks up as an underling enters with important news? Is the light cascading through an open window where we can hear bombs going off?

- Has your lead's wife/girlfriend/child died and now he's gone insane?

- Are two men in an argument (Black, Caucasian, Asian, whatever) where one calls the other bitch? Bro? My Niggah?

- Does your script/film use the game of chess as metaphor?

- Is your production company called Starving Artist Productions?

- When a character gets into bed, does the other person in bed open their eyes? Does the awake character then pretend to remain asleep?

- Do you have a character in a bathtub just under the water?

- If indeed your character emerges from a bathtub full of milky white water, are they also gasping for breath? Shocked they didn't drown? Do they knock over a lit white candle? Is there a cat meowing (out of sync) as it's deciding whether or not to join its owner? Are they startled out of their wishful drowning because a phone rings?

- Is your film about a Polaroid that tells the future? Or an elderly Black female psychic?

- Does a subway train fly past your main character as he ponders life?

- Is your main character the black sheep of the family returning home because someone died, had a miscarriage, or has developed Alzheimer's? Does he also NOT know how to cook (bake, help dad in the garage, dress nicely like your sister)? Or does he instead spend most of the time on his cell phone due to his high-profile job, much to his mother's chagrin?

- When having sex, are your characters actually in a position where intercourse is physically possible?
- Is your animated film an homage to Edgar Allan Poe?
- Is there a tall Black man with a bad Jamaican accent telling your white lead to find Jah? Go back to his girl-friend? "Slow down, man"?
- Does your submission box tell us that this is Temp Sound, Temp Music, Rough Cut, Not Necessarily Picture Locked, Missing Crucial Animated Scenes, and Temp FX?
- When your character is on the phone do they pick it up and listen without saying hello or hang up without hearing or saying goodbye? Do they say they'll be somewhere without disclosing the location or time to meet?
- Is your terrified character (male or female) running through the woods as the camera tracks their feet crunching the debris beneath him or her? Does he or she trip over nothing and fall, crying out in pain as the music picks up the pace, telling us to get scared?
- Are your main characters late for a wedding? Funeral? Does this cause them to fight and the woman to go back to smoking?
- Is the child in the film really the main character at another age, or at the Gates of Heaven?
- Is there a modern dance sequence in your film?
- Are any of the characters in your film a mime?
- A zombie? A robot?
- Is the character in the wheelchair in your film actually wheelchair-bound?

- Is your protagonist coming out of the closet? Do they get beaten up, thrown out of the house, alienated from best friend?

- Does your film have lesbian or gay subtext that never materializes?

- Does anybody commit suicide in your film?

- If you had a quarter for every time one of your characters said "What should we do?" would you have enough money to make your next short?

- Is your short an homage to the silent film era? Complete with Charlie Chaplin lookalike?

- Is anybody in your film being chased due to mistaken identity?

- Did your sound guy put clinking ice in your dinner scene when it's obvious to the audience that there isn't ice in any of the glasses?

- Assuming this isn't a porn short, are any of the women in your film not wearing a bra? In broad daylight?

- Is there a crane shot in your film?

- Does your film feature "the silent homeless guy"?

- Are there white guys in their twenties sitting around a table doing lines of cocaine?

- Does a gun appear out of nowhere, especially when it is obviously fake?

- Did your DP use the old dolly/zoom combo? It worked in *Vertigo*, leave it alone.

- Does a couple break up over a conversation at a café?

- Does your film feature a time-lapse montage?

- Does your main character stare into the bathroom mirror?

- Is there a close-up of water dripping from a faucet?

- Is there a close-up of a clock ticking?

- Is your opening credit sequence almost as long as the film?

- Does your film repeat itself—do I get to see the beginning scene at the end . . . as if I might have memory issues?
- Has the actor you have smoking in your movie ever smoked a cigarette before in his or her life?
- Are there four guys driving to Vegas and one of them accidentally dies?

What? There's More?
Filmmaker Resource Guide

The breadth of resources available to short filmmakers is astounding, particularly online. Steven Tagle (www.steventagle .com) is a great filmmaker, frequent contributor to Current TV, and has been a faithful intern on this book. I asked him to do some research and what he came up with was nothing short of brilliant.

Together, he and I have combed the world over, and below is an extensive list—truly a great place for you to start. Of course, we may have missed one of your favorite Web sites, so by all means send me an e-mail (www.robertamunroe.com), and I'll be sure to add it to my Web site database and any future editions of this book. The Top International Short & Short Friendly Film Festivals list is courtesy of programmer Laurent Crouzeix of the Clermont-Ferrand Short Film Festival in France.

TOP INTERNATIONAL SHORT & SHORT FRIENDLY FILM FESTIVALS

25 FPS Festival
http://www.25fps.hr/08.php
Zagreb, Croatia—feature experimental shorts

Brest European Short Film Festival
http://www.filmcourt.fr
France—European shorts only

Brussels Short Film Festival
http://www.courtmetrage.be
Belgium

Clermont-Ferrand International Short Film Festival
http://www.clermont-filmfest.com
France

Corona Cork Film Festival
http://www.corkfilmfest.org
Ireland

Curtocircuito International Short Film Festival
http://www.curtocircuito.org
Spain

Durban International Film Festival
http://www.ukzn.ac.za/cca/Durban_International_Film_Festival
.htm
South Africa

Encounters Short Film Festival
http://www.encounters-festival.org.uk
UK

Era New Horizons International Film Festival
http://8ff.eranowehoryzonty.pl/index.do
Poland—feature animation and experimental shorts

FESPACO
http://www.fespaco.bf
Ouagadougou, Burkina Faso—Africa.
Happens every two years—2009, 2011, etc.

The Hamburg International Short Film Festival
http://festival.shortfilm.com
Germany

IndieLisboa–International Independent Film Festival
http://www.indielisboa.com
Portugal

Jeonju International Film Festival
http://eng.jiff.or.kr
South Korea

Nordisk Panorama–5 Cities Film Festival
http://www.nordiskpanorama.com
Sweden

Internationale Kurzfilmtage Oberhausen
http://www.kurzfilmtage.de
Germany

Pyongyang International Film Festival
http://www.pyongyanginternationalfilmfestival.com
North Korea & Beijing, China

Short Film Festival in Drama
http://www.dramafilmfestival.gr/index.html
Greece

Short Shorts Film Festival & Asia
http://www.shortshorts.org
Japan

Siena International Short Film Festival
http://www.cortoitaliacinema.com
Italy

Tampere Film Festival
http://www.tamperefilmfestival.fi
Finland

Vila do Conde Shorts
http://www.curtasmetragens.pt
Portugal

SHORT & SHORT FRIENDLY FILM FESTIVALS (U.S. & INT'L)

168 Hour Project
http://www.168project.com
Glendale, CA

Action/Cut Short Film Competition
http://www.actioncut.com/sfc/competition.htm
Studio City, CA

Africa In The Picture
http://www.africainthepicture.nl
Amsterdam, The Netherlands

Angel Film Festival
http://www.angelfilmfestival.org
London, UK

American Indian Film Festival
http://www.aifisf.com
San Francisco, CA

Arizona State University Art Museum Short Film and Video Festival
http://asuartmuseum.asu.edu/filmfest/index.html
Tempe, Arizona

Athens International Sci-Fi and Fantasy Short Film Festival
http://www.alef.gr/english/index.html
Attiki, Greece

Atlantic International Film Festival
http://www.atlanticfilm.com
Halifax, Nova Scotia, Canada

Beverly Hills Shorts Festival
http://www.beverlyhillsshortsfestival.com
Beverly Hills, CA

BijouFlix
http://www.bijoucafe.com
Online

Black Lily Film and Music Festival
http://blacklilyfilm.org
Philadelphia, PA

Break
http://www.break.com
Online

Brooklyn Independent Cinema Series
http://www.brooklynindependent.com
Brooklyn, NY

Brooklyn's Independent Film Theater
http://www.brooklynindiehouse.com
Brooklyn, NY

Canberra Short Film Festival
http://silversunpictures.com.au/csff
Canberra, Australia

Cannes–Short Film Corner
http://www.shortfilmcorner.com
Cannes, France

Cathedral Arts Festival Short Film Festival
http://www.gracevanvorst.org
Jersey City, NJ

CFC Worldwide Short Film Festival
http://www.worldwideshortfilmfest.com
Ontario, Canada

Cleveland International Film Festival
http://www.clevelandfilm.org
Cleveland, OH (note: offers LGBT programming)

Con-Can Movie Festival
http://en.con-can.com
Online

CrankCookieShortfilmdays
http://www.crankcookiekurzfilmtage.de
Passau, Germany

Dam Short Film Festival
http://www.damshortfilm.org
Boulder City, NV

Dawson City International Short Film Festival
http://www.dawsonfilmfest.com
Yukon, Canada

DC Shorts Film Festival
http://www.dcshorts.com
Washington, DC

The Director's Cut
http://www.thedirectorscut.org
New York, NY

The Doorpost Film Project
http://www.thedoorpost.com
Nashville, TN

Dragon*Con Independent Short Film Festival
http://filmfest.dragoncon.net
Atlanta, GA

EarthDance: The Short-Attention-Span Environmental Film Festival
http://www.earthdancefilms.com
Oakland, CA

Elliot Rocke Mudfest
http://www.mudfest.com.au
New South Wales, Australia

Encounters Short Film Festival
http://www.encounters-festival.org.uk
Bristol, UK

FAIF International Short Film Festival
http://www.magicalfilmfest.com
Garden Grove, CA

Frameline–San Francisco LGBT Film Festival
http://www.frameline.org
San Francisco, CA

Film Your Issue
http://www.filmyourissue.com
New York, NY

First Nations Film and Video Festival (USA)
http://www.fnfvf.com

First Sundays Short Comedy Film Festival
http://www.firstsundays.com
New York, NY

Flickerfest (Sydney, Australia)
http://flickerfest.com.au

From Here to Awesome
http://www.fromheretoawesome.com
Online

FW: Fwd
http://www.fwfwd.org
Online

GIAA (Italian) Festival of Short Films and Videos
http://www.giaafilmfest.com
New York, NY

Girona Film Festival
http://www.gironafilmfestival.com
Girona, Spain

Hamburg International Short Film Festival
http://festival.shortfilm.com
Hamburg, Germany

Harmony Film Festival
http://harmonyfilmfest.com
Sydney, Australia

Hamburg Lesbian & Gay Film Festival
http://www.lsf-hamburg.de/content/view/49/86
Hamburg, Germany

Head to Head Online Short Film Competition–World of India
http://www.areyouupforthechallenge.com
Tampa, FL

Hero Fest–My Hero Short Film Festival
http://www.myhero.com/myhero/go/filmfestival/ff_index.asp
Laguna Beach, CA

Huesca Film Festival
http://www.huesca-filmfestival.com
Huesca, Spain

Hull International Short Film Festival
http://www.hullfilm.co.uk
Hull, UK

Image Out–Rochester Lesbian & Gay Film & Video Festival
http://www.imageout.org
Rochester, NY

Independent Lens Online Shorts Festival
http://www.pbs.org/independentlens/insideindies/shortsfest
Online

The Indie Short Film Competition
http://www.indieshortfilms.net
Fort Lauderdale, FL

Inside Out–Toronto LGBT Film Festival
http://www.insideout.on.ca
Toronto, Canada

LA Shorts Fest
http://www.lashortsfest.com
Los Angeles, CA

London Lesbian & Gay Film Festival
http://www.bfi.org.uk/llgff
London, UK

Short Film Festival of India–21st Century Films
http://www.shortfilmfestivalofindia.com
Guwahati and Chennai, India

Mandurah Short Film Festival
http://www.mandurahshortfilmfestival.com
Western Australia, Australia

Manhattan Short Film Festival
http://www.msfilmfest.com
New York, NY

Media That Matters Film Festival
http://www.mediathatmattersfest.org
New York, NY

Miami LGBT Film Festival
http://www.mglff.com
Miami, FL

MisCon Short Film Festival
http://www.miscon.org/Video/index
Missoula, MT

Nashville Film Festival
http://www.nashvillefilmfestival.org
Nashville, TN (note: offers LGBT programming)

National Neighborhood Day Short Film Contest
http://www.neighborhoodday.org
Providence, RI

Narrative Shorts Film+Video Festival
http://www.csuchico.edu/art/galleries/Call%20for%20Entries.htm
Chico, CA

NewFest–New York LGBT Film Festival
http://www.newfest.org/cgi-bin/iowa/index.html
New York, NY

Neversink Valley Area Museum Silent Short Film Competition
http://www.neversinkmuseum.org/filmfest.htm
Cuddebackville, NY

New Filmmakers
http://www.newfilmmakers.com
New York, NY

Open APPerture Short Film Festival
http://www.appfilmfest.com
Boone, NC

Out In Africa–LGBT Film Festival
http://www.oia.co.za
Cape Town, South Africa

Outfest–Los Angeles LGBT Film Festival
http://www.outfest.org
Los Angeles, CA

Palm Springs International Festival of Short Films
http://www.psfilmfest.org
Palm Springs, CA

Pen and Brush–Women in the Arts
http://www.penandbrush.org/events.htm
New York, NY

Really Big Short Film Festival
http://www.reallybigshortfilmfestival.org
Indianapolis, IN

Renderyard Short Film Festival
http://www.renderyard.com
London, UK

Roger Ebert's Film Festival
http://www.ebertfest.com
Champaign, IL; distribution; festival
(Note: There is no submission process. All films are selected
from among the films Mr. Ebert sees in the normal course of
his reviewing).

Sapporo International Short Film Festival and Market
http://www.sapporoshortfest.jp
Sapporo, Japan

San Francisco International Festival of Short Films
http://www.sfshorts.org
San Francisco, CA

São Paulo International Short Film Festival
http://www.kinoforum.org/index_en.htm
São Paulo, Brazil

Science Fiction Short Film Festival
http://www.empsfm.org/programs/index.asp?categoryID=216
Seattle, WA

Seattle LGBT Film Festival
http://www.seattlequeerfilm.com
Seattle, WA

ShakeShock.com Short Film Festival
http://www.shakeshock.com
Los Angeles, CA

Short Circuit–A Short Film Festival
http://www.shortcircuit.com.pk
Karachi Sindh, Pakistan

Short Circuit–Traveling Film Festival
http://www.southarts.org/shortcircuit
Atlanta, GA

Short Cuts
http://www.shortcuts.in
Hyderabad, India

Show Me Shorts Film Festival
http://www.showmeshorts.co.nz
Auckland, New Zealand

Show Off Your Shorts Film Festival
http://www.soysfilmfest.com
Beverly Hills, CA

Shorts Film Festival
http://www.shortsfilmfestival.com
Adelaide, Australia

Short Shorts Film Festival & Asia
http://www.shortshorts.org
Japan and Los Angeles, CA

Standing Rock International Short Film and Video Festival
http://www.standingrock.net
Kent, OH

The Student Shorts Film Festival
http://www.studentshorts.com
Ontario, Canada

Sunnyside Shorts Film Festival
http://www.sunnysideshorts.net
Sunnyside, NY

Taos Shortz Film Fest
http://www.taosshortz.com
Taos, NM

Tehran Short Film Festival
http://www.shortfilmfest.ir/index-en.htm
Tehran, Iran

Tirana International Film Festival
http://www.tiranafilmfest.com
Tirana, Albania

United Nations Association Film Festival
http://www.unaff.org
Stanford, CA

Uppsala International Short Film Festival
http://www.shortfilmfestival.com
Uppsala, Sweden

Webcuts–Internet Film Fest Berlin
http://www.webcuts.org/2007/index_en.html
Berlin, Germany

Winnipeg Aboriginal Film Festival
http://www.aboriginalfilmfest.org
Winnipeg, Manitoba, Canada

Women in Film Festival, B.C.
http://www.wiffbc.com
British Columbia, Canada

Wyllie O Hagan St. Patrick's Day Digital Short Film Festival
http://www.wyllieohagan.com
London, UK

Wyoming Short Film Contest
http://www.filmwyoming.com
Cheyenne, WY

Yorkton Short Film and Video Festival
http://www.yorktonshortfilm.org
Yorkton, Canada

Zinebi
http://www.zinebi.com/eng/universal/home.html
Bilbao, Spain

SHORT FILM DISTRIBUTION

Arab Film Distribution
http://www.arabfilm.com
online; distribution; catalog
> Arab Film Distribution provides American and Canadian
> theaters, universities, colleges, museums, and media centers with
> Arab films of high artistic and educational value.

Atom
http://www.atom.com
> For independent creators, Atom is a pipeline to the big time.
> They license and develop content, pay real money, and distribute
> to huge audiences on the Internet, television, and mobile phones.
> Their partners include Comedy Central, Spike TV, Verizon, and
> BellSouth. Atom is a service of MTV Networks. Located in San
> Francisco.

Big Film Shorts
http://www.bigfilmshorts.com
online; distribution; catalog
> Big Film Shorts is a film distribution company that specializes in
> short films, as well as other media and formats.

BitTorrent
http://www.bittorrent.com
> BitTorrent is the global standard for delivering high-quality files

over the Internet. Their new site, BitTorrent.com, has been launched to provide a better digital entertainment experience for the community of over 150 million users who use their software. With thousands of newly released movies, TV shows, music tracks, and popular PC games available for download, you can easily find what you want, when you want it. BitTorrent even enables you to publish your own content. If you are a filmmaker, musician, or even a comedian, it's the perfect place to showcase your work to a worldwide audience. Located in San Francisco.

B-Side
http://www.bside.com
online; distribution; festival; viral

B-Side is an entertainment technology company that captures audience opinions to discover great films and deliver them to viewers around the world. B-Side discovers films through audience feedback from its community of hundreds of film festival Web sites representing the world's largest film focus group. B-Side delivers these films globally through bside.com and partnerships with distributors including the Independent Film Channel.

Breakthrough Distribution
http://www.breakthroughdistribution.com
online; distribution; services

Breakthrough Distribution was formed in April 2006 to help filmmakers and other content creators maximize their distribution possibilities via online, retail, theatrical, broadcast, and other channels.

ClickPopMedia
http://www.clickpopmedia.com
online; distribution; services

ClickPopMedia is a full-service marketing and advertising group from Nazareth, Pennsylvania. They employ a staff of top-notch designers, ace programmers, and tip-top marketing geniuses.

here! TV Networks
http://www.heretv.com

Founded in 2002, here! airs on all major U.S. cable systems as a 24-hour subscription service. here! appears in 96 of the top 100 U.S. markets, including every top-ten market. here! also was the first gay network originating in the U.S. to launch in Canada.

(Please be advised: here! does not directly accept unsolicited creative ideas or materials. Creative materials should be sent to a literary agency, as all submissions to here! must come through an agent.)

IndieFlix

http://www.indieflix.com
online; distribution; catalog

IndieFlix is the do-it-yourself marketplace for festival-screened and internationally produced content (exceptions are made upon approval) where independent filmmakers from around the world are encouraged to be both artist and entrepreneur, create and promote their work, and be the drivers of their own success.

iTunes

Contact Person: Go to Web site to submit podcasts.
http://www.apple.com/itunes

iTunes is a store, a player, and a way to get music and more on your computer, iPod, iPhone, and Apple TV. Located in Cupertino, CA.

Joost

http://www.joost.com

Joost is packed with Internet tools such as instant messaging and channel chat, allowing people to really share the TV experience. It's a completely secure platform for content owners that respects their rights, while protecting and enhancing their brands. And it's an incredibly flexible way for advertisers to reach a truly global audience, in ways that really work. Located in Leiden, London, New York, and Luxembourg.

Logo (Viacom's LGBT TV channel)

Contact Person: shortfilm@logoonline.com (Please include your name, e-mail address, phone number, and a brief synopsis of your short film.)
http://www.logoonline.com

The LGBT world has a place all its own with Logo, the new lesbian & gay network from MTV Networks. Whether it's on TV, online, or on your mobile, Logo brings you the stories, shows, and news you won't see anywhere else. From original series and films to groundbreaking documentaries to LGBT news and more. Located in New York.

Mini Movie

http://www.minimovie.com

Mini Movie Channel presents a high-quality interactive movie experience to comedy fans. MiniMovie.com features hundreds of professionally created short comedy films licensed from top talent, as well as a host of eye-catching original productions. Headquartered in Beverly Hills, with offices in Luxembourg, Paris, and Moscow, MiniMovie discovers the best short film comedies from around the globe and delivers them via an easy-to-use interface.

Movieola

http://www.movieola.ca

Movieola—The Short Film Channel presents the very best of action, drama, and comedy films that can all be enjoyed in under 40 minutes. From celebrated Academy Award® and global film festival winners to cult favorites, Movieola—The Short Film Channel gives viewers an opportunity to experience the excitement, energy, and emotion of cutting-edge entertainment through the world of short films. Located in Toronto, Canada.

PlaceVine

http://www.placevine.com

online; distribution; marketing

PlaceVine is a dynamic brand integration meeting place connecting an expanding universe of filmed entertainment to relevant, creative marketers. PlaceVine provides new opportunities for content producers to receive logistical and financial support and a new channel for marketers to pursue targeted product exposure. When leveraged properly, we believe that brands can significantly enhance visual context and character development. PlaceVine's mission is to facilitate structured collaboration between the film and marketing communities, resulting in targeted, organic marketing placements.

Shorts International

Contact Person: Linda Olszewski (linda@shortsinternational.com) or Simon Young (simon@shortsinternational.com)

http://www.britshorts.com

Shorts International is a full-service short film entertainment company representing over 3000 films to over 120 international broadcasters across every platform and every medium. The company's catalog includes award-winning, celebrity-driven

premium titles from film festivals around the world as well as
the American Film Institute (AFI), USC, the Hypnotic catalog.
This diverse catalog features both domestic and international
films in their original language. The company has been providing
tailored programming and stellar service to blue chip entertainment companies in Television, Broadband/Internet, Airlines,
Home Video, and Mobile Phones as well as popular consumer
brands. Some examples of their partners include the Sundance
Channel, Canal Plus France, HBO Latin America, Turner/TNT,
Fox Networks Italy, MTV, SVT Sweden, SBS Australia to name a
few. Located in London, New York, Los Angeles, and Paris.

Spout

http://www.spout.com

online; distribution; reviewing

Spout allows you to review films and promote your own film.
They make it easy for people to share movies they love with
others so that the big movie/little movie playing field will be
level and really meaningful stories will find their audience.

Strand

http://www.strandreleasing.com

Strand Releasing was formed in 1989 and its goal has been to
fuse quality art films with commercial product. Strand Releasing
was honored with a ten-year retrospective at New York's Museum
of Modern Art curated by Laurence Kardish. Subsequently, the
Laemmle Theatres in Los Angeles and the Philadelphia International Film Festival hosted similar programs. Partners Jon
Gerrans and Marcus Hu were honored with a lifetime achieve-
ment award for Strand Releasing's accomplishments in 2002
from Outfest. Located in Culver City, CA.

TLA

http://www.tlavideo.com

One of the largest video Web sites in the United States, TLA
features the online sale of American Independent, International,
Hollywood Hits, Gay & Lesbian, and Adult DVD and VHS. The
Web site also offers clothing and gifts, books and CDs.

TubeMogul

http://www.tubemogul.com

online; distribution; services

TubeMogul is the first online video analytics and distribution company serving publishers large and small who need independent information about video performance on the Internet and automated upload to the Web's top video sharing sites.

Wolfe Video

Contact Person: Jeffrey Winter (jeffrey@wolfereleasing.com)
http://www.wolfevideo.com

Wolfe is a premier distributor of gay and lesbian feature films. "We take pride in the fact that, for retailers, producers and consumers, the Wolfe logo on a film attests to its quality, presentation and entertainment value. We value that trust, and have built our business on that strong foundation since 1985." Located in San Jose and Los Angeles, CA.

Women Make Movies

http://www.wmm.com
online; distribution; catalog

Women Make Movies is a multicultural, multiracial, non-profit media arts organization which facilitates the production, promotion, distribution and exhibition of independent films and videotapes by and about women.

BLOGS

Brian Chirls

http://www.chirls.com
online; blog; distribution

Self-prolaimed "Indie Nerd Filmmaker (Director, Distributor, Technologist)" develops and writes about ways for independent artists to create and distribute their work.

CinemaTech

http://cinematech.blogspot.com
online; blog; technology

CinemaTech focuses on how new technologies are changing cinema—the way movies get made, discovered, marketed, distributed, shown, and seen. (With occasional forays into other parts of the entertainment economy.)

Film Festival Secrets
http://filmfestivalsecrets.blogspot.com
online; blog; distribution
> Some genius information about film festivals, the application
> process, and marketing.

A Filmmaker's Life
http://filmmakerslife.blogspot.com
online; blog; craft
> Award-winning filmmaker Jacques Thelemaque describes the
> daily life of an independent filmmaker.

John August
http://www.johnaugust.com
online; blog; screenwriting
> Screenwriter John August answers reader-submitted questions
> about craft.

Power to the Pixel
http://www.powertothepixel.com
online; blog; craft
> Power to the Pixel is a not-for-profit company that provides the
> independent film community with the latest in-depth informa-
> tion and knowledge about new opportunities available in the
> transforming digital media landscape.

Shortsville
http://shortsville.typolis.net
online; blog; distribution
> A blog where short filmmakers sign up to post their stuff daily.

videos.antville.org
http://videos.antville.org
online; blog; distribution
> A blog where users sign up to post cool music videos daily.

COMMUNITY

Black Film Research Online
http://blackfilm.uchicago.edu
> Black Film Research Online (BFRO) is a resource guide for the
> study of Black film culture. We define Black film culture quite

broadly to include the works of Black filmmakers from across the African Diaspora; the production, distribution, and exhibition of films by, for, and about Blacks; issues of Black spectatorship and reception; and images of Black people in film from the invention of the medium in the late nineteenth century to the present.

Chlotrudis Society for Independent Film
http://www.chlotrudis.org
Jamaica Plain, MA; community, distribution; craft, festival
The Chlotrudis Society for Independent Film is a non-profit organization that teaches people to view films actively, helps people experience the world through independent film, and encourages discussion and discourse about film and the world. They run a yearly short film festival in Boston.

DV Info Net
http://www.dvinfo.net
online; community; resource
Online digital video discussion groups where you can post questions and get answers and advice from real people.

Echo Park Film Center
http://www.echoparkfilmcenter.org
Los Angeles, CA; community; craft
Echo Park Film Center is a non-profit media arts organization located in the Echo Park neighborhood of Los Angeles. You can watch a movie, take a filmmaking class, rent a projector, telecine your home movies, check out their extensive film and book lending library, submit your film for programming, buy some Super 8 film, sign up for a membership, or just drop by and say hello!

Filmmakers Alliance
http://www.filmmakersalliance.org
online; community; craft
Started in 1993 as a collective answer to the practical needs of independent filmmakers, Filmmakers Alliance has evolved into a multi-layered support organization with an emphasis on aesthetic empowerment.

Film Independent
http://www.filmindependent.org
Los Angeles, CA; community; craft

Film Independent is a non-profit organization dedicated to independent film and independent filmmakers. Our 6,300 members have access to discounted equipment, editing suites, casting rooms, a valuable resource library, over 120 free screenings, and 150 educational events every year.

Fundable Online Fundraising
http://www.fundable.com
online; community; fundraising

Fundable.com lets groups of people pool funds to make purchases or raise money. Each Fundable project has a description of how much money needs to be collected and what it will do. Once enough pledges (not payments) have been collected, Fundable turns them into real payments and sends the total to the project's organizer.

Hanksville–Native American Video Resource List
http://www.hanksville.org
online; community; database

Harvard Independent Film Group
http://www.harvardfilmgroup.com
Cambridge, MA; community; craft

The Harvard Film Group regularly invites leading writers, directors, actors, and industry leaders to discuss their personal experience. They have frequent live readings and screenings of new work.

Independent Feature Project
http://www.ifp.org
online; community; resource

IFP is a 30-year-old, not-for-profit membership and advocacy organization that supports and serves the independent film community by connecting creative talent and the film industry. Wide-reaching programs provide invaluable information, resources, networking, and support to filmmakers while promoting film as a vital and influential public art form. Located in New York, NY.

IndieGoGo
http://www.indiegogo.com
online; community; fundraising

IndieGoGo is an online social marketplace connecting filmmakers and fans to make independent film happen. The platform provides filmmakers the tools for project funding, recruiting, and promotion, while enabling the audience to discover and connect directly with filmmakers and the causes they support.

Inner-City Filmmakers

http://www.innercityfilmmakers.com

Los Angeles, CA; community; craft

Inner-City Filmmakers is a non-profit organization dedicated to opening doors for low-income high school seniors by providing free year-round professional and business training, mentors, and paid work opportunities in the motion picture and television industries.

LoftCity

http://www.loftcity.com

online; community; craft

LoftCity is the world's first online film studio. Our vision is to create a global community of professional filmmakers who can come together to share ideas, collaborate and showcase new work. We provide a platform for professional filmmakers from all disciplines within the industry to produce high quality professional Web and mobile films.

La Lutta NMC

http://www.lalutta.org

San Francisco, CA / New York, NY; community; craft

La Lutta New Media Collective (NMC), a non-profit, community-based organization, is a diverse group of people united to promote a greater level of social awareness through new media.

Meetup

http://www.meetup.com

online; community; craft

Meetup is the world's largest network of self-organized clubs and community groups. Search for "film" in your city, and you're bound to find groups that share your interests.

MySpace Film

http://www.myspace.com/index.cfm?fuseaction=film

online; community, distribution; viral

A division of the popular social networking Web site where filmmakers can create profiles and upload their films.

Raindance

http://www.raindance.co.uk

London, UK; community, education, distribution; craft; festival

Since 1992 Raindance has been offering advice and support for independent fimmakers. They started the Raindance Film Festival in 1993, and the British Independent Film Awards in 1998. They also have a training program that has had remarkable success. Presently there are nine people working out of their office in Soho, London. "Although we are London-based we are on the look-out for anyone who might like to work with us in another city or country."

Script Frenzy

http://www.scriptfrenzy.org

online; community; screenwriting

Script Frenzy is an international writing event in which participants attempt the daring feat of writing 100 pages of scripted material in the month of April.

Shooting People

http://www.shootingpeople.org

online; community; craft; resource

Shooting People is a community of 37,000+ filmmakers who share their resources, skills and experience. Members post to and receive up to eight daily e-mail bulletins, which cover all aspects of filmmaking; add their events and screenings to the Indie Film calendars; and network with other members at parties, salons and screenings in London, New York and beyond; create dynamic, online searchable profile cards; and upload their films and reels to the site.

StudentFilmmakers.com

http://www.studentfilmmakers.com

online;community; database; craft; resource

StudentFilmmakers.com and StudentFilmmakers Magazine's Social Networking Community is dedicated to aspiring film and video makers of all ages and levels around the world.

TriggerStreet.com

http://www.triggerstreet.com

online; community; screenwriting

TriggerStreet.com was founded by Kevin Spacey in January 2002 as the Web-based filmmaker and screenwriter's community of record—an interactive mechanism for the purpose of discovering and showcasing new and unique talent. Based on the principles of creative excellence, it provides industry access and exposure to help build the careers of notable new filmmakers and screenwriters of our day.

Women in Film and Television Vancouver

http://www.womeninfilm.ca

Vancouver, Canada; community; craft

Women in Film and Television Vancouver (WIFTV) is an internationally affiliated non-profit society committed to advancing and celebrating women in screen-based media.

Videomaker

http://www.videomaker.com

online; community; craft; resource

Videomaker empowers people to make video in a way that inspires, encourages and equips for success; we do this by building a community of readers, Web visitors, viewers, attendees and marketers.

DATABASES & RESOURCES

Action-Cut-Print!

http://www.actioncutprint.com

online; database; resource

Action-Cut-Print! is Peter D. Marshall's monthly newsletter and online resource center for filmmakers. Peter is constantly adding new film and TV resource links, creating new filmmaking articles, presenting filmmaking workshops and keeping you up-to-date on film festivals and movie reviews.

Box Office Report

http://www.boxofficereport.com

online; database; resource

Box Office Report tracks box office records all the way back to 2000.

Casting Call Pro

http://www.castingcallpro.com

online; database; cast

Welcome to Casting Call Pro the online casting call solution for actors, presenters, agents and casting professionals. Whether you

work in theater, radio, television and film, or corporates, Casting
Call Pro is here to help. Listing the very latest in acting jobs,
auditions, and casting calls.

Celtx

http://www.celtx.com
online; database; services

Celtx is the world's first fully integrated solution for media
pre-production and collaboration. It replaces old-fashioned
"paper, pen & binder" media creation with a digital approach to
writing and organizing that's more complete, simpler to work
with, and easy to share. This is the one my Inner-City Filmmaker
students use.

Cinema Sites

http://www.cinema-sites.com
online; database; resource

Cinema Sites lists film and television resources available on the
Net. Often, the links are annotated, and the most important
pages of a specific site automatically come forward onto the
Cinema Sites main page.

Clipland

http://www.clipland.com
online; database; resource

Clipland was founded in late 1998 to provide the most comprehensive database of music video details and rare background
information. To achieve this ambitious aim, Clipland was
designed as an open database where every interested user can
submit his own piece of information and share it with the world.
Now Clipland is also the movie-trailer database, commercial
database, and more.

craigslist

http://www.craigslist.org
online; database; cast; crew

Online classifieds that you can use to find actors, crew members,
equipment. Located worldwide—check to see if your city is
listed.

Creative Commons–Legal Music for Videos

http://creativecommons.org/legalmusicforvideos
online; database; resource

Many musicians choose to release their songs under Creative Commons licenses, which give you the legal right to do things like use their music in your videos.

Creative Handbook
http://www.creativehandbook.com
Los Angeles, CA; database; resource
> The ultimate LA production resource guide to help you sift through the many production-related companies and services available in Southern California.

EntertainmentCareers.net
http://www.entertainmentcareers.net
online; database; crew
> Entertainment jobs, internships, and career information in the entertainment industry.

FameCast
http://www.famecast.com
online; database; artist
> FameCast is the premier artist discovery engine that collects, ranks, and serves up the world's best emerging artists for entertainment fans and industry professionals in search of new talent.

Film Festival World
http://www.filmfestivalworld.com
online; database; distribution
> The FFW Network creates a context for FFW members to connect and collaborate with others who produce, program, write about, and distribute films and new media.

indieWIRE
http://www.indiewire.com
online; database; news
> Celebrating its tenth anniversary, indieWIRE is the leading news, information, and social networking site for the international independent film community, including comprehensive coverage of indie, documentary, and foreign-language films, as well as industry news, film festival reports, filmmaker interviews, and movie reviews. I have their newsletter delivered to my inbox *every day.*

The Internet Movie Database (IMDb)

http://www.imdb.com

online; database; film

> The Internet's free, fully searchable film and TV credit database.
> This is one of the most comprehensive databases out there,
> listing details on every film and filmmaker in recorded history.

Ken Stone's Final Cut Pro

http://www.kenstone.net/fcp_homepage/fcp_homepage_index.html

online; database; editing

> A comprehensive Final Cut Pro database.

LA Casting

http://www.lacasting.com

Los Angeles, CA; database; cast

> LA Casting is a free online casting database for Los Angeles.

Mandy's Film and TV Production Directory

http://www.mandy.com

online; database; cast; crew

> A free database of international film and TV resources, including
> casting calls, production jobs, vendors, film markets, and
> classified ads. Located in U.S.A.

Media-Match

http://www.media-match.com

online; database; crew

> Media-Match is an online database of over 30,000 Film and TV
> professionals' resumes and availability, and an up-to-date jobs
> board for new openings in the TV and Film production business
> across the United States.

Now Casting

https://www.nowcasting.com

Los Angeles, CA; database; cast

> Now Casting is a free online actors database and electronic
> submissions service based in LA.

Pixar Shorts

http://www.pixar.com/shorts

online; database; craft

> A collection of short films created by Pixar.

ProductionHUB

http://www.productionhub.com

online; database; resource; cast; crew

ProductionHUB, Inc. is the leading online resource and industry directory for film, television, video, and digital media production. Developed as a tool for people to locate production products, services, and professionals, ProductionHUB has grown to become the number one production search engine. Over 200,000 monthly users rely on ProductionHUB to deliver up-to-date information related to the production industry.

SF Casting Networks

http://www.sfcasting.com

San Francisco, CA; database; cast

SF Casting is a free online casting database for the Bay Area.

Streaming Video

http://www.streamingvideos.com

online; database; craft

Streaming Video contains a variety of articles about how best to film and edit streaming videos for the Internet.

The StudioSystem

http://www.studiosystem.com

online; database; film

The StudioSystem is an entertainment, film, and television database, providing subscribers with detailed information on the people, projects, and companies engaged in the development, production, release, and performance of film and television content.

UNLV Short Film Archive

http://shortfilmarchive.unlv.edu

online; database; craft; festival

The goal of the UNLV Short Film Archive is to establish a comprehensive collection of significant short films from all over the world from the beginning of filmmaking to the present. The cornerstone of the archive will be the Archive 100, the one hundred most significant shorts, culturally, historically, or aesthetically, selected by an international panel of film historians, recognized film festival programmers, film producers, directors, distributors and recognized short film scholars.

USC School of Cinematic Arts

http://www-cntv.usc.edu

Los Angeles, CA; education; craft

Including a directory of film-related businesses, individuals, and organizations, this site originates from the nationally famous film school. It features an electronic mall and message board.

Withoutabox

http://www.withoutabox.com

online; database; festival

Allows filmmakers to search for film festivals worldwide and submit their films electronically.

The Workbook Project

http://www.workbookproject.com

online; database; craft

Their goal is to create a free resource for content creators that will become a user contributed repository of information.

SCREENWRITING DATABASES & COMPETITIONS

American Gem Short Screenplay Competition

http://www.filmmakers.com/contests/short

Mission Viejo, CA; distribution; competition; short script

Short screenplay, teleplay, stage play, or animation. Submissions must be narrative short film, 3–45 pages in length, in any genre, possible to produce on a low budget.

BeingCharlieKaufman.com

http://www.beingcharliekaufman.com

online; database; screenwriting

A Charlie Kaufman fansite that features drafts of all his scripts.

BlueCat Screenplay Competition

http://www.bluecatscreenplay.com

Los Angeles, CA; distribution; competition; short script

Now in its tenth year, the BlueCat Screenplay Competition has discovered more successful writers and provided more support through our analysis and feedback to more writers than any screenplay competition in the world. This is one of my favorite sites—Gordy Hoffman and Heather Schor will rock your world.

Drew's Script-O-Rama
http://www.script-o-rama.com
online; database; screenwriting
My favorite script database—links to hundreds of shooting scripts and transcripts for feature films

The Internet Movie Script Database
http://www.imsdb.com
online; database; screenwriting
The biggest collection of movie scripts available anywhere on the Web. This site lets you read or download movie scripts for free.

Screenwriting.info
http://www.screenwriting.info
online; database; screenwriting
This overview will acquaint you with screenwriting format rules and etiquette.

SimplyScripts
http://www.simplyscripts.com
online; database; screenwriting
A screenwriter's resource with links to hundreds of free downloadable movie scripts, screenplays, and transcripts of current and classic films and TV shows.

BROADCAST & ONLINE TELEVISION

Atom
http://www.atom.com
online; distribution; viral
Atom is a daily source of original Web shows, animation, and short films. They license and develop content, pay real money, and distribute to huge audiences on the Internet, television, and mobile phones. A loyal supporter of independent filmmakers and animators, Atom has built a platform for its artists looking for

worldwide distribution. The company selects fewer than
10 percent of the hundreds of shorts they review each month.

Aussie Short Films

http://www.aussieshortfilms.com.au
Australia; distribution; viral; catalog

Aussie Short Films offers a selection of the best dramatic and
educational films in our drama section. Absurd and innovatively
crafted light entertainment in comedy. And a window on
Australia in documentary. "Our aim is the creation of a professional microcinema specializing in Australian short films.
Some of our content will always be free, but sound commercial
practices will enable us to endure while similar Web sites come
and go."

Babelgum

http://www.babelgum.com
online; distribution; viral

Babelgum is here to offer you a wide range of fascinating content,
with an emphasis on the original and the unconventional.

Bebo

http://www.bebo.com
online; distribution; viral

Bebo is a social media network where friends share their lives
and explore great entertainment.

BitTorrent

http://www.bittorrent.com
online; distribution; viral

BitTorrent.com launched to provide a better digital entertainment experience for the community of over 150 million users
who use our software. BitTorrent even enables you to publish
your own content. If you are a filmmaker, musician, or even a
comedian, it's the perfect place to showcase your work to a
worldwide audience.

blinkBox

http://www.blinkbox.com
online; distribution; viral

At blinkBox you can watch, buy, and rent movies and TV shows.
blinkBox features fantastic stuff from big and small producers

alike, and blinks, the ability to clip your favorite part, personalize it, and use it as you wish.

blip. tv
http://www.blip.tv
online; distribution; viral

> A great service for great shows. A new class of entertainment is emerging that is being made by the people without the support of billion-dollar multinationals. "Our mission is to support these people by taking care of all the problems a budding videoblogger, podcaster or Internet TV producer tends to run into. We'll take care of the servers, the software, the workflow, the advertising and the distribution. We leave you free to focus on creativity."

Brightcove
http://www.brightcove.com
online; distribution; viral

> Brightcove is an Internet TV platform dedicated to harnessing the inherent power of the Internet to transform the distribution and consumption of media.

Channel 4 Shorts
http://www.channel4.com/film/shortsandclips/shorts.html
online; distribution; viral

> This site features ten of UK Channel 4's favorite short films.

Crackle
http://www.crackle.com
online; distribution; viral

> Crackle, Inc., a Sony Pictures Entertainment Company formerly known as Grouper, is a multi-platform video entertainment network and studio that distributes the hottest emerging talent on the Web and beyond.

Current TV
http://www.current.com
online; TV station; viral

> Current pioneered the television industry's leading model of interactive viewer created content (VC2). Comprising roughly one-third of Current's on-air broadcast, this content is submitted via short-form, non-fiction video "pods." Viewer Created Ad Messages (VCAMs) are also open to viewers participation. Offers filmmaker training and resources as well.

Filmaka

http://www.filmaka.com

online; distribution; viral

Filmaka pledges to reward your creativity. Our monthly competitions provide exciting challenges where you can win prizes, showcase your work, develop your skills, and find an audience.

Funny or Die

http://www.funnyordie.com

online; distribution; viral; humor

Funny or Die is a comedy video Web site that combines user-generated content with original, exclusive content. Ridiculously funny—I've spent many hours laughing at old SNL skits featuring Will Ferrell.

Joost

http://www.joost.com

online; distribution; viral

Joost combines the best things about television—great shows, great picture quality, something that everyone knows how to use—with the incredible power of the Internet to bring people together and deliver entertainment on demand.

maniaTV

http://www.maniatv.com

online; TV station; viral

The maniaTV Network launched in 2004 as the world's first Internet television network. The company produces, sells and distributes made for Internet programming targeting the 18-to-34-year-old audience.

Mefeedia

http://www.mefeedia.com

online; distribution; viral

Mefeedia allows users to search across 15,000 video sources.

Mini Movie Channel

http://www.minimovie.com

online; distribution; viral

Mini Movie Channel presents a high-quality interactive movie experience to comedy fans. MiniMovie.com features hundreds of professionally created short comedy films licensed from top talent, as well as a host of eye-catching original productions. Headquartered in Beverly Hills, with offices in Luxembourg, Paris and Moscow, MiniMovie discovers the best short film comedies from around the globe and delivers them via an easy-to-use interface.

MovieFlix

http://www.movieflix.com
online; distribution; viral; catalog

Welcome to MovieFlix.com! We've got the largest selection of movies on the Internet with thousands of titles to choose from! MovieFlix has hundreds of shorts and other first-run content, as well as movie merchandise, articles, box office figures, and more. Contact MovieFlix about submissions. Requires Real Player.

Movieola

http://www.movieola.ca
online; distribution; viral

Movieola—The Short Film Channel gives viewers an opportunity to experience the excitement, energy and emotion of cutting-edge entertainment through the world of short films.

MySpace TV

http://vids.myspace.com
online; distribution; viral

A division of the popular social networking Web site, MySpace TV allows users to upload short content.

The New Venue

http://www.newvenue.com
online; distribution; database; viral; resource; craft

The New Venue is an arbiter of quality, presenting the most innovative "new movies for a new medium" to a world-wide media-savvy community. It features short indie films which break aesthetic and technical barriers, bringing story and style to the Internet and to the Palm O.S. It also empowers digital filmmakers with "FlickTips," the complete guide to making Web movies.

OurStage

http://www.ourstage.com

online; distribution; viral

> OurStage is where the world's music fans come to discover, enjoy and reward the best emerging artists—and where the world's artists come to find their fans, get amazing gigs, and launch their careers.

Raindance TV

http://www.raindance.tv

online; distribution; viral

> Raindance TV delivers the best in independent filmmaking via high-quality, streaming video direct to your PC or Mac, including the best feature films, shorts and documentaries from the Raindance Film Festival—Britain's largest independent film festival.

Revver

http://www.revver.com

online; distribution; viral

> Revver is a video-sharing platform built the way the Internet really works. "We support the free and unlimited sharing of media. Our unique technology tracks and monetizes videos as they spread virally across the Web, so no matter where your creativity travels, you benefit."

Spike

http://www.spike.com

online; distribution; viral

> Spike gives guys what they want and a voice that is unapologetically male. A leading destination Web site, Spike.com serves user-uploaded and professional content to over ten million viewers monthly. "Our extensive library includes movie clips, music videos, short films, TV, clips, video game trailers, action sports, and a popular 'viral videos' collection."

Studentfilms.com

http://www.studentfilms.com

online; distribution; database; festival; resource

> Studentfilms.com's mission is to be the ultimate filmmaking resource for film students. Showcase your student short film on the site and receive valuable feedback from your peers. The site's discussion forums are perfect for advice on shooting that perfect

film, getting into film school, finding a composer, and much
much more.

Sundance Film Festival–Online

http://www.sundance.org
online; distribution; viral

Every year Sundance showcases the shorts in the festival. Make
sure to sign up for their podcast for free on iTunes and sign up
for their newletter on their Web site.

Ustream TV

http://www.ustream.tv
online; distribution; viral

In just minutes, you can broadcast and interact with a global
audience from one to thousands! All it takes is a camera and an
Internet connection.

Veoh

http://www.veoh.com
online; distribution; viral

Veoh is a revolutionary Internet TV service that gives viewers the
power to easily discover, watch, and personalize their online
viewing experience.

Vuze

http://www.vuze.com
online; distribution; viral

Vuze is the world's most popular entertainment platform for
high-res digital content: video, music, and games.

Wonderland

http://www.wonderlandstream.com
online; distribution; viral

Looking Glass: The guide where a filmmaker membership
features the best movies on the Web. "Filmmakers choosing
filmmakers."

YouTube

http://www.youtube.com
online; distribution; viral

Founded in February 2005, YouTube is the leader in online video,
and the premier destination to watch and share original videos
worldwide through a Web experience. YouTube allows people to

easily upload and share video clips on www.YouTube.com and across the Internet through Web sites, mobile devices, blogs, and e-mail.

Zango

http://www.zango.com

online; distribution; viral

Zango, Inc. is an online media company providing consumers free access to a large catalog of free, sought-after online videos, games, music, tools, and utilities.

Index

Angela Brinskele

Roberta Munroe is a filmmaker and film consultant. She has been a director of programming and programmer at film festivals across the country and, of course, programmed the acclaimed short film program at the Sundance Film Festival for five years. As a director, she was accepted into the Fox Searchlight Directors Program (*foxsearchlab*) and has made two award-winning short films, *Dani and Alice* and *Happy Birthday*, that have played at more than 150 film festivals worldwide and gained distribution deals on iTunes and through Wolfe Video. She has been on several panels and juries, including Toronto Worldwide Short Film Festival, Big Bear Lake International Film Festival, Palm Springs ShortFest, NewFest, and the University of North Carolina School of Filmmaking. Roberta has mentored students at Inner-City Filmmakers for four years and was recently named one of *GO* magazine's 100 Women We Love. Roberta lives in Echo Park, Los Angeles, California, with her rescued Miniature Pinscher, Marcello.